A PRACTICAL GUIDE TO COUNSELING THE GIFTED IN A SCHOOL SETTING

SECOND EDITION

Joyce VanTassel-Baska
Editor

A product of the ERIC Clearinghouse on
Handicapped and Gifted Children

The Council for Exceptional Children

Library of Congress Cataloging-in-Publication Data

A Practical guide to counseling the gifted in a school setting.
 "A product of the ERIC Clearinghouse on Handicapped and Gifted Children."
 Includes bibliographical references.
 1. Gifted children—Education. 2. Personnel service in education. I. VanTassel-Baska, Joyce. II. ERIC Clearinghouse on Handicapped and Gifted Children.
LC3993.2.P7   1989   371.95   89-25413
ISBN 0-86586-192-7

A product of the ERIC Clearinghouse on Handicapped and Gifted Children

Published in 1990 by The Council for Exceptional Children, 1920 Association Drive, Reston, Virginia 22091-1589.
First Edition 1983. Second Edition 1990
Stock No. 268   Price $12.50

This publication was prepared with funding from the U.S. Department of Education, Office of Educational Research and Improvement, contract no. RI88062007. Contractors undertaking such projects under government sponsorship are encouraged to express freely their judgment in professional and technical matters. Prior to publication the manuscript was submitted to The Council for Exceptional Children for critical review and determination of professional competence. This publication has met such standards. Points of view, however, do not necessarily represent the official view or opinions of either The Council for Exceptional Children or the Department of Education.

Printed in the United States of America.
10 9 8 7 6 5 4 3 2 1

Contents

About the Authors v

1. Introduction 1
   Joyce VanTassel-Baska

2. Recent Trends and Issues in Counseling the Gifted 6
   Joyce VanTassel-Baska

3. Issues in Affective Development of the Gifted 15
   Linda Kreger Silverman

4. Who Should Counsel the Gifted:
   The Role of Educational Personnel 31
   Beverly Ness Parke

5. Collaboration of Teachers and Counselors in Serving
   Affective Needs of Gifted Students 40
   Joyce VanTassel-Baska

   Appendix to Chapter 5—A Small Group Counseling
   Unit for Gifted Elementary Students 54

6. The Parent's Role in Counseling the Gifted:
   The Balance Between Home and School 57
   Arlene Munger

7. School Counseling Needs and Successful Strategies
   to Meet Them 66
   Joyce VanTassel-Baska

8. The Writing, Reading, and Counseling Connection:
   A Framework for Serving the Gifted 72
   *Jane M. Bailey, Linda Neal Boyce,
   and Joyce VanTassel-Baska*

9. Educational Therapy for the Gifted:
   The Chicago Approach 90
   Leland K. Baska

10. A Model for Counseling the Gifted at the
    High School Level 96
    Ron Seegers

This monograph is affectionately dedicated to the memory of

Margaret Bynum,

A tireless advocate of the needs of the gifted for almost a quarter century in her beloved Georgia. The field of the education of the gifted shall miss her leadership at the national level where she served CEC-TAG and other organizations so admirably.

Ave atque vale, carus amice.

About the Authors

Jane M. Bailey, Ed.S., is currently a coordinator of the LIBRARIES LINK LEARNING Project for The College of William and Mary's Center for Gifted Education. She has directed the William and Mary summer gifted learner programs and has taught writing process courses.

Leland Baska, M.Ed. and M.S., was a school psychologist with the Chicago Public Schools for 18 years, the last 12 exclusively with gifted children. More recently he has been a school psychologist with the Williamsburg, James City-County Schools and now does contract testing and consulting in the Tidewater region of Virginia.

Linda Neal Boyce, M.L.S., has been a public school and academic librarian. She currently coordinates library services for the LIBRARIES LINK LEARNING Project for The College of William and Mary's Center for Gifted Education and teaches children's literature at Christopher Newport College.

Arlene Munger, Ed.D., was formerly the director of programs for the gifted in the state of Indiana and is past president of the Indiana Federation of The Association for the Gifted (TAG). She is retired and living in Florida.

Beverly Ness Parke, Ph.D., is associate professor in special education at Wayne State University, Detroit, Michigan. In addition to her work in evaluation of gifted programs and teacher training, Dr. Parke has taught and served as consultant to gifted programs nationally. She is President of CEC-TAG.

Ron Seegers, M.A., has been director of programs for the gifted in the Homewood-Flossmoor High School District, Flossmoor, Illinois, since 1978. He also serves as chairman of the social science department of the high school and is very active in statewide activities in gifted education.

Linda Kreger Silverman, Ph.D., is director of the Gifted Child Development Center in Denver, Colorado. She has worked extensively with gifted children and their parents in counseling

About the Authors
(Continued)

and testing over the last 20 years. She also teaches courses on counseling the gifted in addition to other teacher training activities.

Joyce VanTassel-Baska is The Jody and Layton Smith Professor of Education at The College of William and Mary and directs The Center for Gifted Education there. Prior to her current role, she has served as a local, state, regional, and university director of gifted programs in the Midwest. She has published extensively in the education of the gifted, particularly on the topics of curriculum, counseling, and the disadvantaged gifted. She is a former president of The Association for the Gifted (TAG).

CHAPTER ONE

Introduction

Joyce VanTassel-Baska

This guide is to serve as a reference for personnel without specific training in counseling and guidance but with the responsibility for the education of gifted children in counseling as well as in the areas of curriculum and instruction. It is organized to provide an overall sense of direction for beginning a counseling program component for gifted students. Initially, we look at the differential affective characteristics and needs and some of the associated issues and problems. Next, we attempt to define counseling roles and functions for various educational personnel who influence the lives of gifted students. The role and function of parents in the total counseling process are also delineated. Alternative strategies for addressing the counseling needs of gifted students are then presented for implementation by teachers of the gifted. We conclude with the presentation of two model counseling programs, one in a large urban area and one in a suburban setting. Figure 1 illustrates the progression and flow of these developmental topics in counseling the gifted.

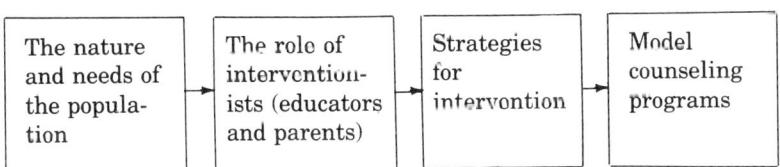

Figure 1. A flowchart of developmental topics in counseling the gifted.

This editor and those who contributed chapters believe that some form of counseling and guidance is necessary for the full development of potential in gifted students and should be carried out by individuals sensitive to the affective characteristics and needs of the gifted population. In most school settings, those individuals are classroom teachers, teachers of the gifted, or program coordinators and specialists whose full-time job function is working directly with gifted children. It is to these people that this monograph speaks.

A PRACTICAL DEFINITION

Most common textbook definitions of counseling and guidance would dichotomize the two terms into a collection of clinical psychosocial issues that would constitute counseling, and a collection of educational and career issues that would constitute guidance. For the purposes of this monograph, no such distinctions exist. The terms *counseling* and *guidance* will refer to the processes employed to help gifted students develop as whole persons within the context of the school setting. In that sense, then, both affective and cognitive concerns require the assistance of a "wise friend." The need to present gifted students with opportunities for informed choice in all aspects of their lives lies at the crux of this conception of counseling and guidance.

LONG-TERM BENEFITS

Those who may read this guide seeking a "recipe," or a formula for "what to do in the affective domain with the gifted for 30 minutes on two mornings a week" will be disappointed. The counseling ideas explored may not be easily translated into specific activities for classroom application. Rather, the advice rendered reflects a need to develop an understanding about facilitating gifted students' affective growth over time. Thus, many of the approaches advocated are long term, with student benefits being viewed as cumulative and developmental.

However, there is a great need for personnel in gifted education to work with parents and others in the school community to understand the affective differences of gifted students and provide direction accordingly. A teacher of the gifted can often be the best "translator" of gifted behavior that a student has. We hope that educational personnel reading this guide will internalize the need for their professional involvement and help in working with the gifted population in the counseling domain even though they have not been trained as counselors per se.

DIFFERENCES IN GIFTED STUDENTS

Perhaps it is most important to understand the differences among gifted children in respect to their need for special counseling and guidance and the timing regarding its provision. No two children are exactly alike, particularly in respect to personality and emotional make-up. Many gifted students encounter no difficulty with establishing social relationships. Others, particularly the highly gifted, may find this a difficult area. Some gifted students are naturally gregarious; others may prefer to pursue solitary endeavors. Some gifted students are very self-confident and secure in their ability; others lack self-esteem to the extent that underachievement patterns can develop. Therefore, an appropriate counseling approach must take into account such individual differences among the gifted.

AN INTEGRAL PART OF PROGRAMS

Implicit within this monograph is the assumption that counseling and guidance should be integral components of a program for gifted students, to be addressed as a part of program treatment rather than apart from it. While many school districts offer academic programs for the gifted, very few offer the commensurate counseling experiences that will aid students in developing holistic self-understanding. Advocacy for addressing the confluence of cognitive and affective needs in gifted students through developmental counseling is essential.

GUIDING PRINCIPLES

A set of guiding principles derived from the research and practice noted in the chapters that follow may be useful as a beginning reference to this guide. The term "counselors of the gifted" is used here to refer to those personnel willing to provide the support system needed for the gifted student, not necessarily those trained in counseling procedures or functioning in the role of counselor:

1. Counselors of the gifted should be attuned to differences in the emotional as well as the intellectual systems of gifted students and work with students based on these differences (Piechowski, 1974; Silverman, Chapter 3, this volume).
2. Counselors of the gifted should help these students learn about their special characteristics so that feelings of being different, of

social alienation, and of inferiority are not allowed to develop unchecked (Sanborn, 1979; Webb, 1981).
3. Counselors of the gifted should focus on both cognitive and affective needs of gifted students through a program that provides academic, psychosocial and career counseling experiences (VanTassel-Baska, 1981; Chapter 7, this volume).
4. Counselors of the gifted should act as advocates for the gifted student in the educational institution and help negotiate and facilitate individual progress through appropriate school experiences (Parke, Chapter 4, this volume).
5. Counselors of the gifted should provide an information clearinghouse for outside resources that could benefit these students. Human resource needs include role models and mentors; material resource needs might be in the area of museums, libraries, and universities (Munger, Chapter 6, this volume).
6. Counselors of the gifted should aid students in decision-making skills and planning. These students tend to have more choices in regard to course-taking, college, and careers than do other students and frequently need to make decisions earlier in their school careers. (Gowan, Demos, & Kokaska, 1965; Hoyt & Hebeler, 1974; Seegers, Chapter 10, this volume).
7. Counselors of the gifted should value, encourage, and reward self-initiated learning on the part of students (Gowan et al., 1965).
8. Counselors of the gifted should develop a system for assessing tested strengths and weaknesses of individual students and providing constructive criticism for developing a plan of action around them (Stanley, Keating, & Fox, 1974).
9. Counselors of the gifted should encourage students to read books that relate to their particular problems or situations and should provide a reading list and follow-up discussion opportunities. Such bibliotherapy techniques have been found to be most effective for counseling this population (Fraser & McCannon, 1981).
10. Counselors of the gifted should be sensitive to the value conflicts experienced by students who come from low socioeconomic backgrounds. Such students need special support and help in clarifying their goals and moving toward actualizing them (Gowan et al., 1965; Gowan & Bruch, 1971).
11. Counselors of the gifted should establish a special network of female students in order to encourage course-taking in mathematics and science as well as to provide support for high-level academic decisions (Fox, Brody, & Tobin, 1980).
12. Counselors of the gifted should act as chief communicators to other educational personnel on individual case problems or gen-

eral issues regarding the needs of these students (Baska, Chapter 9, this volume).

13. Counselors of the gifted should serve as initiators in the identification process of these special students whether for inclusion in special programs or for individual attention from others in the education community (Colangelo & Zaffrann, 1979; Perrone & Male, 1981).
14. Counselors of the gifted should team with parents, psychologists, and others who influence these students to conduct "staffings" on severe problems related to underachievement, social adjustment, or personal crises. Referral to outside agencies or specialists in such cases may be appropriate (Gowan & Bruch, 1971; Colangelo & Zaffran, 1979).

REFERENCES

Colangelo, N., & Zaffrann, R. T. *New voices in counseling the gifted.* Dubuque IA: Kendall/Hunt, 1979.

Fox, L. H., Brody, L., & Tobin, D. (Eds.). *Women and the mathematical mystique.* Baltimore MD: Johns Hopkins University Press, 1980.

Frasier, M. M., & McCannon, C. Using bibliotherapy with gifted children. *Gifted Child Quarterly,* 1981, *25* (2), 81-85.

Gowan, J. C., & Bruch, C. B. *The academically talented student and guidance.* New York: Houghton-Mifflin, 1971.

Gowan, J. C., Demos, G. D., & Kokaska, C. J. *Guidance of exceptional children.* New York: David McKay, 1965.

Hoyt, K., & Hebeler, J. *Career education for gifted and talented students.* Salt Lake City UT: Olympus, 1974.

Perrone, P. A., & Male, R. A., *The developmental education and guidance of talented learners.* Rockville MD: Aspen Systems, 1981.

Piechowski, M. M., Two developmental concepts: Multilevelness and developmental potential. *Counseling and Values,* 1974, *18,* 86-93.

Sanborn, M. P. Counseling and guidance needs of the gifted and talented. In A. Harry Passow (Ed.), *NSSE yearbook: The gifted and talented.* Chicago: University of Chicago Press, 1979.

Stanley, J. C., Keating, D. P., & Fox, L. H. *Mathematical talent.* Baltimore MD: Johns Hopkins University Press, 1974.

VanTassel-Baska, J. A comprehensive model of career education for gifted and talented. *Journal of Career Education,* 1981, *7,* 325–331.

Webb, J. *Counseling the gifted.* Columbus: Ohio Psychology Press, 1981.

CHAPTER TWO

Recent Trends and Issues in Counseling the Gifted

Joyce VanTassel-Baska

In the school context, the status of counseling gifted students has probably not changed very much since the initial publication of this guide (VanTassel-Baska, 1983). However, there have been important developments in the counseling literature, in clinical practice, and in other settings with the gifted that deserve commentary. These developments may be characterized as:

- Greater emphasis on counseling families and parents of the gifted.
- Focus on the treatment of specific problems of the gifted such as underachievement and perfectionism.
- Recognition of counseling needs based on the developmental level of the gifted student under consideration; for example, a whole literature is evolving on counseling the gifted adolescent.
- Counseling centers at universities that specialize in working with gifted children and their parents.
- Self-help publications that guide students, parents, and teachers in providing assistance on coping with giftedness.

The evident paucity of formal school counseling programs and services may also stem from another more prevalent phenomenon, namely teachers taking on the role of counselors with gifted learners at all stages of development and incorporating counseling strategies and activities into their curricular plans. This development, alluded to in the original publication (Parke, 1983), is treated more broadly in two chapters in this edition.

GREATER EMPHASIS ON COUNSELING FAMILIES AND PARENTS OF THE GIFTED

Although schools may not be incorporating formal counseling programs for the gifted very quickly, informally they are providing information to parents regarding the need for counseling through selected parent education programs. Such information encourages many parents of the gifted to seek professional counseling, either from individuals in private practice or from universities offering counseling programs. The primary model used for family counseling is the family systems model (Hackney, 1981), which recognizes the gifted child as part of a larger social network.

In addition to family counseling on psychosocial issues in raising a gifted child, there has been a real interest in counseling families regarding educational planning. Questions such as the following are routinely discussed with parents to help them choose an appropriate school for their child:

1. What is the philosophy/policy on self-pacing and flexibility regarding age/grade placement?
2. What is the philosophy/policy on grouping able learners together for special instruction (multi-age, etc.)?
3. What is the quality of the teaching staff at subsequent grade levels (K–3; 4–6; 7)?
   - Knowledge of subject matter
   - Flexible management style
   - Not intimidated by able students
4. Does the school value individuation as much as or more than socialization?
5. Is there a written curriculum guide and how is it used?
6. Are there adequate support services geared to the needs of gifted learners as well as handicapped learners?
7. Is administrative staff flexible in respect to change of teacher/ program for a given child?
8. How is academic talent recognized and rewarded?

Moreover, helpful lists on evaluating a classroom for young children are available:

1. What are the skill-based expectations of the program? (Are children expected to recognize and write numbers 1–20?)
2. Is homework expected, and if so, what kind?
3. How is discipline handled?
4. Are there special resource people for art, music, library, etc.?
5. In order to understand the curriculum purpose, ask, "What are your objectives for teaching that subject?" (For example: French, or memorizing the Presidents of the United States.)
6. Is the program individualized so that the teacher can work one-on-one?
7. Are there enough adults to work with the group? Is there at least one teacher and an assistant with every group, so that if one is busy with a particular child, the other is responsible for the group? (One adult for every 9 children is recommended, with no more than 20 in a class.)
8. Can children make choices? (Of centers, art projects, colors, etc.)
9. Are parents involved? Are you encouraged to visit the program, or talk to the staff about your child's growth?
10. What is the philosophy regarding curriculum? Is it centrally prescribed teacher-developed, or textbook-based? (Ask for a curriculum guide.)
11. How varied are the activities in a given day? Ask for a schedule of morning and afternoon activities. How much free time and play time is in the schedule?
12. Is there use of cooperative learning groups or small groups that focus on a particular topic of interest?
13. Do the teachers appear flexible in how they organize the classroom and work with children? Do they enjoy bright children?
14. Can children be grouped by ability rather than just age for academic work?
15. How are early academics handled in the school? Are reading and math perceived as skills only or broad areas for learning?
16. What is done in science and social studies? Are students given opportunities for experimentation? Are students exposed to geography?
17. Are children allowed to learn skill-based activities at their own rate (e.g., children working at different levels in a reading or

math program based on diagnostic placement according to level)?
18. How do the principal and teachers articulate outcomes for able learners based on participation in classes at pre-K through Grade 1 levels?

Excellent resources are available for parents and gifted students interested in receiving help with selecting colleges, applying for scholarships, and career opportunities (Berger, 1989). Test-taking services are also available in many areas of the country to assist in the tutorial work necessary to boost SAT or ACT scores so as to gain entrance to more prestigious institutions.

UNDERACHIEVEMENT AND PERFECTIONISM

Key problems of the gifted such as underachievement and perfectionism have been raised to the level of treatable maladies through counseling over the last several years. These problems have been addressed separately in key resources (Adderholdt-Elliott, 1987; Rimm, 1986; Whitmore, 1980) and have also spawned a fair amount of clinical work. Unfortunately, the research base regarding these areas is not much better defined than it was 10 years ago except for promising work in the area of hidden disabilities (Daniels, 1983; Fox, Brody, & Tobin, 1983; Whitmore & Maker, 1985). Yet clinical practice has continued to observe and work on these areas as central problems for many gifted learners. Some schools have even established separate programs for gifted underachievers. Suggested interventions with this population include:

- One-to-one counseling.
- Conducting activities to build self-esteem.
- Analyzing major strengths and arranging participation in activities that build on them.
- Helping the student set goals and initiate follow-up behavior.
- Offering learning opportunities based solely on interest.
- Providing college and career guidance.
- Providing real-world experiences in an area of potential career interest.
- Setting up tutorials in areas of the curriculum where the student needs assistance.

- Using creative problem solving to motivate the student.
- Employing safe "risk taking" situations.

COUNSELING THE GIFTED ADOLESCENT

Adolescence has always been considered a critical stage of development for all students, not just the gifted. In the 1980s, however, counseling gifted adolescents has become increasingly prevalent. Spawned in part by the nationwide talent searches which identify gifted learners at 12 to 14 years of age, adolescent counseling became an adjunct to the service delivery function of these search models. The Midwest Talent Search at Northwestern University, for example, has developed a counseling model for disadvantaged adolescent students and their families from the city of Chicago. The program has several components:

1. *Seminars.* Parents are invited to special "parent" seminars covering topics on:
    - Providing emotional support for the college-bound student.
    - College financing.
    - Letting go—for the parent apprehensive about the distance between home and college.
    - What college life is all about—for the parent who desires updated information on today's college campuses.
2. *Internships* give students an opportunity to work with an adult professional on a day-to-day basis and learn more about career options. *Mentorships* provide students with additional guidance and insight into a profession and with assistance in the college admissions process.
3. *Workshop Series.* In the third year, a workshop series focuses on personal skills:
    - Study skills and habits.
    - Time management.
    - Decision making.
    - Goal setting.
    - Note taking.

Moreover, research on adolescent coping mechanisms has revealed that gifted learners use coping strategies that differ from those used by typical adolescents (Buescher, 1987). A key study of adolescent behavior (Csikszentmihalyi & Larsen, 1985) documented important differences between high-achieving and low-achieving adolescents in their use of leisure time. High-achieving students spent leisure time in productive and constructive activities, whether alone or with others, while low-achieving students spent time "hanging out," socializing with friends, or watching television. The study also presented important data on family contexts that best nurture motivation. The family context variables cited by Csikszentmihalyi include:

- Choice and control over activities.
- Clarity of rules and feedback.
- Centering on intrinsic process and rewards.
- Commitment, involvement, security, trust.
- Challenge through providing various opportunities for action.

These insights from the literature lend support to the current emphasis on counseling gifted adolescents yet also carry implications for the need for earlier intervention. A set of studies conducted with adolescents at Northwestern University and reported in a key volume focusing on adolescent gifted development (VanTassel-Baska & Olszewski-Kubilius, 1988) further demonstrates the current emphasis in this area.

COUNSELING CENTERS AT UNIVERSITIES

The number of universities with an interest in working with gifted children and their parents has grown exponentially in the 1980s. In an eight-state region of the Midwest, for example, university programs and services for gifted children increased from 24 in 1982 to 65 in 1983. This growth pattern appears to be typical across the country. Some universities, such as the University of Wisconsin and the University of Nebraska, have specialized in counseling services for the gifted. Furthermore, some have a specific counseling focus; for example, the new center at the University of Iowa specializes in career counseling of the gifted.

These specialized settings are also contributing a new research base around counseling the gifted. A large-scale study was conducted, for example, among high school seniors taking the ACT, to determine college planning issues (Kerr & Colangelo, 1988). It found differential career interests based on aptitude levels, broad interests in participation in extracurricular activities in college, limited interest in personal counseling, and great interest in career planning assistance and college course opportunities. A study of younger adolescents and their parents yielded comparable results regarding the desire for counseling (VanTassel-Baska & Damiani, in press). Counseling needs were perceived to be predominantly in the area of academic planning rather than psychosocial assistance. Yet a study of adolescents at the University of Denver yielded a key list of psychosocial concerns of the gifted (Strop, 1983):

- Feeling different.
- Heightened sensitivity and intensity.
- Perfectionism.
- Feeling inadequate (the imposter syndrome).
- Moral issues and universal concerns (related to intellectual abilities).
- Developing relationships.

SELF-HELP PUBLICATIONS

Materials have been developed to address the issues of coping with giftedness from both children's and parents' perspectives. These materials appear to be widely used by the gifted community both at home and at school. A list of some of the more popular selections follows:

Adderholdt-Elliott, M. (1987). *Perfectionism: What's bad about being too good?* Minneapolis, MN: Free Spirit Publishing.
Delisle, J. R. (1984). *Gifted children speak out.* New York: Walker & Co.
Delisle, J., & Galbraith, J. (1987). *The gifted kids survival guide II.* Minneapolis, MN: Free Spirit Publishing.
Galbraith, J. (1983). *The gifted kids survival guide, for ages 11–18.* Minneapolis, MN: Free Spirit Publishing.
Galbraith, J. (1984). *The gifted kids survival guide, for ages 10 and under.* Minneapolis, MN: Free Spirit Publishing.
Kerr, B. (1985). *Smart girls gifted women.* Columbus, OH: Ohio Psychology Press.
Webb, J., Meckstroth, E., & Tolan, S. *Guiding the gifted child: A practical source for parents and teachers.* Columbus, OH: Ohio Psychology Press.

Two other books provide important insights into the role of parents in "counseling" the development of high-level talent. They are:

Bloom, B. (1985). *Developing talent in young people.* New York: Ballantine.
Feldman, D. (1986). *Nature's gambit.* New York: Basic Books.

Although limited to cases of extraordinary talent (Bloom focuses on individuals who became world class competitors in a specific field by the age of 35 and Feldman on child prodigies), both books provide interesting documentation on the role of parents as coaches, encouragers, and monitors of their child's progress in a given talent area, as well as parents' need for good counsel regarding appropriate instructors and long-term planning.

CONCLUSION

While these developments constitute some positive growth in the area of counseling the gifted, the role of schools in the process still remains somewhat ill-defined. In many school districts the responsibility for counseling gifted students is tacitly given to teachers. Thus the emphasis on affective curriculum as a mode of providing counseling assistance has become common. Chapters 5 and 8 address this issue more fully.

REFERENCES

Adderholdt-Elliott, M. (1987). *Perfectionism: What's bad about being too good?* Minneapolis, MN: Free Spirit Publishing.

Berger, S. (1989). *College planning for gifted students.* Reston, VA: The Council for Exceptional Children.

Buescher, T. M. (Ed.). (1987). *Understanding gifted and talented adolescents: A resource guide for counselors, educators, and parents.* Evanston, IL: Center for Talent Development, Northwestern University.

Csikszentmihalyi, M., & Larsen, R. (1985). *Being adolescent.* Chicago, IL: University of Chicago Press.

Daniels, P. (1983). *Teaching the gifted/learning disabled child.* Rockville, IL: Aspen.

Delisle, J. R. (1984). *Gifted children speak out.* New York: Walker & Co.

Delisle, J., & Galbraith, J. (1987). *The gifted kids survival guide II.* Minneapolis, MN: Free Spirit Publishing.

Fox, L., Brody, L., & Tobin, D. (1983). *Learning disabled gifted children.* Baltimore, MD: University Park Press.

Galbraith, J. (1983). *The gifted kids survival guide, for ages 11–18.* Minneapolis, MN: Free Spirit Publishing.

Galbraith, J. (1984). *The gifted kids survival guide, for ages 10 and under.* Minneapolis, MN: Free Spirit Publishing.

Hackney, H. (1981). The gifted child, the family, and the school. *Gifted Child Quarterly, 25,* 51–54.

Kerr, B. (1985). *Smart girls gifted women.* Columbus, OH: Ohio Psychology Press.

Kerr, B., & Colangelo, N. (1988). The college plans of academically talented students. *Journal of Counseling and Development, 67*, 42–47.

Parke, B. (1983). Who should counsel the gifted: The role of educational personnel. In J. VanTassel-Baska (Ed.), *A practical guide to counseling the gifted in a school setting.* Reston, VA: The Council for Exceptional Children.

Rimm, S. (1986). *Underachievement syndrome: Causes and cures.* Watertown, WI: Apple Publishing.

Schmitz, C., & Galbraith, J. (1985). *Managing the social and emotional needs of the gifted.* Minneapolis, MN: Free Spirit.

Strop, J. (1983). *Counseling needs of the gifted.* Unpublished dissertation. Denver, CO: University of Denver.

VanTassel-Baska, J. (Ed.). (1983). *A practical guide to counseling the gifted in a school setting.* Reston, VA: The Council for Exceptional Children.

VanTassel-Baska, J., & Damiani, V. (in press). Gifted adolescent and parent perceptions of careers and counseling needs. *Roeper Review.*

VanTassel-Baska, J., & Olszewski-Kubilius, P. (Eds.). (1988). *Patterns of influence on gifted learners.* New York: Teachers College Press.

Webb, J., Meckstroth, E., & Tolan, S. *Guiding the gifted child: A practical source for parents and teachers.* Columbus, OH: Ohio Psychology Press.

Whitmore, J. R. (1980). *Giftedness. conflict and underachievement.* Boston: MA: Allyn & Bacon.

Whitmore, J., & Maker, J. (1985). *Intellectual giftedness in disabled persons.* Rockville, MD: Aspen Press.

CHAPTER THREE

Issues in Affective Development of the Gifted

Linda Kreger Silverman

> What can I say about school? It was a way of life for twelve years, a lesson in accommodation and retreat, a pervasive and debilitating servility which the circumstances thrust upon all of us, even the very strongest. It was a few ephemeral brilliances—here a teacher deeply loved, and here another, years later. It was lesions in one's capacity to comfort and to care, the cries of a once friend or a friend-to-be which went unanswered. But most of all it was silence, an illimitable silence which pressed me ever deeper into myself, so that I felt myself growing weaker day by day, growing less human because I was treated as a student, as a thing, not as "she who," but as "it that." "To teach is to love," to learn as well. And we loved each other so little, these others and I. We were creatures of the system; I bowed to the grade, they to the bells and a harsh word from above. We treated each other as functions, Teacher and Student: far easier than to attempt the terrifying leap of the I-Thou, the leap of humanity over void, over sullen gray mornings—over silence.
> I was a good student. I learned my lessons thoroughly... and well. A good student; indeed, a superb student. But not, after all, a model student, because there were too many questions, too many rude hopes piercing the lost, desolate hours, too much rage in the face of fatuity and lies and cruel indifference, too wild a desperation in the attempt to discover what being human in this world could possibly mean for me...

This excerpt was taken from an essay on school written for me by a high school senior. Her cry of outrage against the emotionally barren school environment went unanswered. No one heard. She was lauded as valedictorian, but no one saw or responded to her despair.

While other students were busy trying to master the course material, she was trying to grasp the purpose of her existence.

The depth and intensity in these passages reveal the extent of this young woman's giftedness and creativity. Few students would have her scope of knowledge, her perceptiveness of the impact of social institutions, her sensitivity to the emotional void, her ability to think and express herself in metaphor, her existential conflict, her idealistic vision of the way the world could be, or her intense reaction to the discrepancy between the ideal and the real. These qualities of thought and feeling are unique to the gifted, and they require a unique mode of response from counselors and counselor-teachers.

UNIQUE NEEDS

The intricate thought processes that mark these individuals as gifted are mirrored in the intricacy of their emotional development. Idealism, self-doubt, perceptiveness, excruciating sensitivity, moral imperatives, desperate needs for understanding, acceptance, love—all impinge simultaneously. Their vast emotional range may make them appear contradictory: mature and immature, arrogant and compassionate, aggressive and timid. Semblances of composure and self-assurance often mask deep feelings of insecurity. The inner experience of the gifted young person is rich, complex, and turbulent.

Although we have made inroads in meeting the cognitive needs of the gifted, we have not become as responsive to their affective needs (Treffinger, Borgers, Render, & Hoffman, 1976). Among the reasons suggested for this deficit are the traditional lack of concern in education for the affective domain (Tannenbaum, 1982); the attitude on the part of parents that emotions are to be dealt with in the home rather than in the school (Elgersma, 1981); and the position that if the school meets the child's cognitive needs, affective development will automatically follow (Mehrens & Lehman, 1973).

The problem is exacerbated by the fact that few teachers, counselors, psychologists, or even specialists working with the gifted recognize that gifted students have a unique set of affective needs. In a nationwide study of the extent to which gifted children are recognized and served, U.S. Commissioner of Education Sidney Marland, Jr. found that professionals were not only unaware of the needs of these children, but often hostile toward them.

> Identification of the gifted is hampered not only by costs of appropriate testing...but also by apathy and even hostility among teachers, administrators, guidance counselors and psychologists. (Marland, 1972, p. 3)

PROBLEMS OF GIFTED STUDENTS

There are problems associated with giftedness. Some are external in origin, caused by the lack of acceptance and understanding of giftedness in society. Others are internal, related to developmental advancement, or, perhaps, to a more highly developed central nervous system. The greater awareness, sensitivity, and intensity of experience shown by many gifted people would favor the latter hypothesis. The most frequent issues faced by gifted young people are:

- Confusion about the meaning of giftedness
- Feeling different
- Heightened sensitivity
- Idealism
- Feelings of inadequacy
- Relentless self-criticism
- Increased levels of inner conflict
- Deep concerns with morality and justice
- Lack of understanding from others
- Unrealistic expectations of others
- Hostility of others toward their abilities

The gifted child pays a heavy toll for society's confusion about the nature of giftedness. Definitions of giftedness are so variable that children come to believe that their abilities are situational. "I used to be gifted in elementary school, but I'm not gifted anymore."

Perceptions of Others

Labeling has many negative aspects. Teachers may expect the child to be gifted in everything, and may bludgeon him or her with the label. "If you're so gifted, how come you can't spell?" The child may have to deal with overt or covert hostility from teachers as well as peers.

Parents may also have unrealistic expectations of the child. In some cases, parents become so threatened by the label, "gifted," that they give the child too much responsibility and decision-making power, in effect causing a role reversal in the family (Dirks, 1979). All of these reactions from parents, teachers, and peers make it difficult for the child to gain a healthy perspective on the meaning of giftedness.

In a world where individual differences are not valued, the child who feels different from others suffers, believing, "There's something wrong with me." Some of these fears can be allayed through appropriate counseling at the time of identification. For the child who is never recognized as gifted, or who is recognized, but never told that he or she is gifted, feelings of being unacceptable and inferior to other people can remain a haunting reality, sometimes for an entire lifetime.

Self-Perceptions

Many of the other concerns listed are manifestations of the child's perfectionism or idealism. The ability to perceive what might be, and the tenacity to try to make one's vision a reality, are rare gifts. But they are emotionally costly. Many times well-meaning parents and teachers try to get these children to set "more realistic" expectations for themselves. This is usually ineffective. It is as difficult to cure a perfectionist as it is to create one.

The moral concerns of the gifted are important signs of advanced development. Terman (1925) asserted that the gifted child of 9 or 10 had reached a stage of moral development which is not attained by the average child until the age of 13 or 14. Marland (1972) also found evidence of the early development of moral concerns in the gifted:

> Gifted pupils, even when very young, depart from self-centered concerns and values far earlier than their chronological peers. Problems of morality, religion, and world peace may be troublesome at a very early age. Interest in problems besetting society is common even in elementary-age gifted children (Marland, 1972, p. 16).

The heightened sensitivity shown by these children is an extremely pervasive trait (Silverman, 1982). Unfortunately, they are taught to be ashamed of being "overly" sensitive—particularly boys. This sensitivity is the basis for their compassion, their deeper understandings of morality and justice, their creativity. It also leads to increased levels of inner conflict. The sensitivity and inner conflict are painful, but they are both essential to emotional development. These children need help in understanding these qualities and in honoring them.

Personality Traits and External Factors

In addition to these general areas of concern, gifted children may have specific problems as a result of certain personality traits or external circumstances. Among these difficulties are:

- Difficulty with social relationships
- Difficulty in selecting among a diversity of interests
- Lack of sufficient challenge in schoolwork
- Depression (often manifested as boredom)
- High levels of anxiety
- Difficulty accepting criticism
- Hiding talents to fit in with peers
- Nonconformity and resistance to authority
- Refusal to do routine, repetitious assignments
- Inappropriate criticism of others
- Lack of awareness of impact on others
- Excessive competitiveness
- Isolation from peers
- Low frustration tolerance
- Intolerance of others
- Poor study habits

Generalizations must be made cautiously, as gifted individuals differ from each other more than they resemble each other (Sanborn, 1979). However, it is clear from the array of concerns listed above, and their pervasiveness, that it is difficult to be gifted, especially for young people.

LACK OF RECOGNITION OF SPECIAL NEEDS

Although the importance of specialized approaches to counseling the gifted would seem apparent, the lack of recognition of the specific affective needs of this population has resulted in little conceptualization about appropriate means of serving these needs. In the field of psychology, there is a conspicuous absence of concern for this group. At least 42 divisions of the American Psychological Association currently exist, none of which focuses on the gifted. I was recently asked to complete a survey of specialty areas disseminated by a state psychological association. Every exceptionality was included in the list except giftedness. Counselors and psychologists receive no training on the emotional development of the gifted, nor do they perceive the need for such training.

Even within the field of gifted education, the attention given to counseling needs has been sporadic and superficial. The few books purportedly dealing with this topic devote only a small portion of their contents to counseling. Computer searches on counseling the gifted reveal mostly material on career counseling. Articles which appear to be concerned with the affective development of this group contain an assortment of group activities originally designed for *all* children as a part of affective education. Workshop presentations on this topic take existing counseling theories and practices and apply them to the gifted with little modification. How is it that children of such depth are conceptualized in such a shallow manner?

The lack of recognition of the counseling needs of the gifted is in part due to the fact that the early leaders in the field succeeded in convincing the world that gifted children had fewer emotional problems than others. This was an important contribution, especially in light of the attitudes of the time. At the turn of the century, it was assumed that giftedness was akin to insanity (Lombroso, 1891; Nisbet, 1891). Quetelet, a famous Belgian statistician of the 19th century, expressed the philosophy of his time in the doctrine that the average man is nature's ideal, and that deviations toward the good as well as toward the bad are nature's mistakes (Boring, 1950). Kretschmer (1931) attributed genius to bastardization, the result of the union of unlike elements. Ashamed and frightened of their children's "abnormal" precocity, parents often hid their children's abilities and conscientiously taught them to conform—to be "normal."

Terman (1925–1959) devoted his life to dispelling this tragic myth. He compared the character traits of over 1,000 gifted children with traits of nongifted children, and found gifted children to be above average on all dimensions.

> As compared with unselected children they are more trustworthy when under temptation to cheat; their reading preferences, character preferences, and social attitudes are more wholesome and they score higher in emotional stability. On total score of the character tests, the typical gifted child of nine years tests as high as the average child of twelve (Terman & Oden, 1947, p. 56).

Terman's results were supported by the research of Hollingworth (1942), Lewis (1943), and Witty (1930). Hollingworth studied the highly gifted and found them to be generally superior in emotional health. They did, however, appear to suffer from a deficit in social relationships.

> Such children are ordinarily friendly and gregarious by nature, but their efforts at forming friendships tend to be defeated by the scarcity of like-minded contemporaries (Hollingworth, 1942, p. 302).

Most of the early leaders in the field were concerned with changing the prevalent stereotypes. They studied groups of gifted children and compared them on numerous measures with groups of average children. The only researchers who studied the emotional lives of the gifted in any depth were those, like Hollingworth, who were intrigued with prodigies or the most brilliant of these children.

GUIDANCE: HISTORICAL PERSPECTIVE

The idea of guidance for the gifted was born at Harvard University, in the early 1930's, when John Gowan and John Rothney studied together under the direction of John Brewer and Truman Kelley. Brewer wrote the first book on educational guidance, and Kelley, Terman's statistician, wrote the first doctoral dissertation on educational guidance (Zaffrann & Colangelo, 1977). Gowan and Rothney developed the concept of differentiated guidance for the gifted (Gowan, 1982). Rothney founded the Guidance Laboratory for Superior Students in Madison, Wisconsin. Gowan developed a summer program for gifted children at San Fernando Valley State College, in which counselors and teachers were trained in working with the gifted. Much of the current research on counseling the gifted stems from these two training grounds.

In the half-century since its inception, the branch of counseling dealing with the gifted has made strides in the following areas:

- Understanding underachievement
- Describing characteristics of the creative
- Recognizing the special problems of the culturally diverse
- Calling attention to the plight of gifted women
- Developing career counseling programs

However, we still lack a theory of affective development: a theory which takes into account the unique intellectual and emotional characteristics of the gifted; a theory upon which to base sound, differentiated counseling practices.

THEORY OF EMOTIONAL DEVELOPMENT

A theoretical construct is emerging which may serve as a needed foundation for counseling the gifted. Dabrowski's Theory of Emotional Development offers a promising framework for understanding the emotional needs of the gifted.

Kazimierz Dabrowski (1902–1980), a Polish psychiatrist and psychologist, formulated the theory while studying gifted, creative, and eminent individuals. He discovered that what appeared to the psychiatric community as symptoms of "psychoneurosis" were often the hallmarks of higher level emotional development (Dabrowski, 1972). Dabrowski viewed the depth of sensitivity, intensity, perfectionism, inner conflict, feelings of inadequacy, depression, and existential anxiety that he saw in his most creative clients as signs of developmental progress, processes propelling these individuals toward higher levels of functioning.

Levels of Human Functioning

In his theory, Dabrowski described five distinct levels of human functioning, ranging from egocentrism at Level I, group domination at Level II, self-examination at Level III, self-actualization at Level IV, and attainment of the personality ideal at Level V. Individuals at Level I experience little inner conflict, self-reflection or empathy for others. Their aims in life are either self-preservation or self-aggrandizement. They are emotionally limited, with little capacity or desire to respond to the emotional needs of others. The rigidity of their convictions and prejudices reflects the rigidity of their psychological composition.

In Level II, the rigidity is replaced with an overabundance of flexibility. The individual is adrift with no rudder in a sea of choices. All paths appear to be of equal value. Society has its greatest impact at Level II. External standards, imposed by the social group, form the basis for judgment in the absence of internal standards. The individual tends to feel inferior to others or to have grave concerns about how he or she is perceived by others.

Since it is the most socialized of the levels, Level II can be thought of as "normal development." There is a wide range of manifestations of Level II. At the lower end of the spectrum, there is an ongoing battle between egocentrism and orientation toward others. At the upper end, the individual struggles to overcome external domination and establish an autonomous identity. A great deal of inner conflict may exist, often with a theme of "my needs vs. their needs."

Level III is marked by the individual's emerging awareness of a personality ideal and the compelling need to measure himself or herself against this ideal. The recognition of lower and higher elements in oneself leads to a struggle between "what is" and "what ought to be." The struggle involves moral questioning, existential concerns, and self-judgment directed toward the discovery and actualization of a universal hierarchy of values (Greene, 1982). There is far-reaching psychological transformation, and sensitivity to more universal and essential problems of humanity. Here one is not concerned with one's identity but with one's place in the universe and one's responsibility to a larger universal community. It is the Level III characteristics that are least understood by the psychological community.

Level IV can be most easily understood as similar to Maslow's level of self-actualization. The struggle between "what is" and "what ought to be" is transformed into "what ought to be, will be" (Dabrowski & Piechowski, 1977). Individuals at Level IV show high levels of responsibility, authenticity, reflective judgment, empathy for others, autonomy of thought and action, self-awareness, self-control, and inner psychic transformation.

Level V is the attainment of the personality ideal, the ultimate in human evolution. At this level, the individual lives in harmony with universal principles of justice.

Most of the world functions at Levels I and II. Each level is more human and more humane than the preceding level. At each succeeding level, there are fewer and fewer individuals. To be adjusted, accepted and understood often means to remain at Level II, the level of the norm. To evolve beyond the confines of social normality may mean social isolation.

Gifted young people often have much stronger personal values than their peers. They tend to be more sensitive to others and more aware of injustice in the world. I have often seen Level III characteristics in gifted adolescents. The essay that began this chapter exemplifies many of these traits. The young author writes of the "terrifying leap of the I-Thou," a metaphor for the transformation to a universal set of values which would compel us to see our responsibility to all of humanity. She berates herself, as well as her teachers, for treating others as functions, because she perceives her own potential to function at a higher level.

Overexcitabilities

Another facet of Dabrowski's Theory is the concept of "overexcitabilities." Overexcitabilities (OE's) are heightened sensitivities to various kinds of stimuli which create tension within the nervous system. Dabrowski (1938) identified five forms of psychic overexcitability: psychomotor, sensual, intellectual, imaginational, and emotional. The psychomotor mode is expressed as a high degree of energy, activity, and movement. The sensual mode involves the capacity for sensory pleasure derived from seeing, hearing, smelling, tasting, and touching. The intellectual mode includes questioning, analysis, problem solving, theoretical thinking, and the capacity for sustained intellectual effort. The imaginational mode is seen as vivid imagery, invention, and the capacity for creative imagination. The emotional mode is expressed as intense feelings, strong attachments to others, self-evaluation and judgment, fear and anxiety, and inhibition (Piechowski, 1979).

The overexcitabilities are the building blocks of the levels: the greater their number and intensity, the greater the "developmental potential"—the potential for higher level development. They are referred to as "overexcitabilities" because these expressions of "excitability" only make a significant contribution to development when they are beyond the normal range (Dabrowski & Piechowski, 1977). Dabrowski (1938) considered the OE's to be innate characteristics, and Piechowski (1979) has shown how these traits can be used to identify the gifted.

> The forms of "overexcitability" are particularly prominent in the gifted and creative because there we find a higher level of energy and capacity for sustained effort (psychomotor OE), enhanced differentiation and aliveness of sensual experience (sensual OE), greater avidity for knowledge, discovery, and attitude of questioning and questing (intellectual OE), greater vividness of imagery, richness of associations, and capacity for detailed visualization (imaginational OE), and greater depth and intensity of emotional life (emotional OE). One may think of these five forms of overexcitability as the substrate of giftedness and creative talent (Piechowski, Silverman, Cunningham, & Falk, 1982).

Studies at the University of Denver have confirmed that gifted adults have high levels of overexcitability in all areas. Particularly important was the finding that emotional OE equalled intellectual OE in an intellectually gifted population (Silverman & Ellsworth, 1980). Similar results were found in a study of gifted adolescents (Piechowski & Colangelo, in preparation). Preliminary studies that I have conducted of gifted children indicate that high levels of emotional OE are present early in life. According to parental reports, gifted children tend to be highly sensitive and compassionate. In one study, 97% of the children ($N = 40$) showed signs of emotional OE (Silverman, 1982).

Giftedness and Emotional Endowment

The results of these studies indicate a linkage between giftedness and emotional endowment. It appears that gifted individuals tend to have high degrees of emotional overexcitability, higher developmental potential, and unique emotional needs. The manifestations of this potential are easily misunderstood, since they might appear as characteristics which the psychological community deems neurotic (Dabrowski, 1972): relentless self-criticism, obsession with one's ideals, depression, vivid reactions to injustice, rejection of a social group whose values are less developed, and deep feelings of inferiority and inadequacy which appear unwarranted.

A COUNSELING FRAMEWORK

Dabrowski's Theory also serves as a counseling framework for gifted and creative individuals. It is most beneficial in terms of the changes in attitude it promotes in both the counselor and the counselee. The counselor comes to view intense inner experiences as positive signs of development, rather than as negative indicators of emotional disturbance. The counselor's role is to reframe the negative attitudes of the counselee toward his or her own experiences. This frees the energy that is being used in self-doubt and self-deprecation, and makes it available for the development of coping mechanisms.

Young people often internalize messages from the society that are counterproductive to healthy emotional development. They are made to feel that they should not have problems or "negative" feelings, such as anger, hurt, or unhappiness. They should not be "overly" sensitive or experience inner conflict. People who experience these things are called "immature," "maladjusted," or, worse, "mentally unstable." When a sensitive gifted child feels a great deal of pain in relation to an incident others see as "trivial," the child may come to perceive himself or herself according to these negative labels. "There is something wrong with me because I feel this way." Well-meaning adults may respond to the child by saying, "Don't *be* that way." If the messages of "Don't be the way you are" are too strong, the young person may become severely depressed, even suicidal.

The sensitive counselor or counselor-teacher can remove much of the anxious overlay, the misperceptions which prevent the child from achieving any degree of self-acceptance. The counselor-teacher validates the child's feelings, helping the child to see that the emotions are healthy. The counselor respects the child's problems, both the nature of the conflicts and the fact that the child has these inner growth experiences. He or she can also intervene with the parents, and with other teachers, if necessary, who do not understand the child's inner world.

Using the Dabrowskian model, the counselor *does not attempt to help the child resolve the problems*. Support is given without taking sides on the issues involved, or all sides of an issue are validated. In this way, the young person is helped to feel that the issues are real and important, rather than trivial and easily resolved by an outsider. The child remains in conflict as long as necessary in order to come to some inner resolution *on his or her own*. The counselor is in no hurry to "cure" the problem, because he or she believes deeply in the value of the conflict for personal growth, and in the child's ability to cope adequately, given time and encouragement.

The developmental significance of inner conflict has been shown by other researchers in addition to Dabrowski. Kohlberg (1973) believes that one must have life experiences involving moral choices in order to develop to the highest levels of moral judgment. When moral dilemmas are presented to the child in a teaching context, the teacher is advised to prolong the discussions to enable the children to experience the dilemmas and to think about them at a deeper level. It would follow that when the child encounters moral choices in real life, the same advice would be appropriate. The less reflection on the problem, the less opportunity for development.

Kohlberg (1975) indicates that parents and teachers can influence moral development by example and by their patterns of interaction. He found that morally advanced children had parents at higher stages, who engaged their children in discussions of moral issues. When real-life models of higher development are scarce, children can be exposed through reading to eminent figures with high moral integrity. Fictional characters can also be used as models. The teacher-counselor can guide the student to books which deal with conflicts similar to the child's. Bibliotherapy can be an asset in nurturing development in the gifted child.

The clearest example of the application of the Dabrowski model in counseling is described in a chapter entitled "Giftedness as Multilevel Potential: A Clinical Example" (Ogburn-Colangelo, 1979) in *New Voices in Counseling the Gifted,* (Colangelo & Zaffran, 1979). The book also contains a chapter on the use of the theory to identify the gifted: "Developmental Potential" (Piechowski, 1979). It was in reading these two articles that I first became aware of the theory.

Since my introduction to Dabrowski's Theory, I have been applying it in my own counseling practice, and I have found the results to be quite positive. Upon exposure to the concepts, clients experience an immense sense of relief and renewed hope. When inner conflicts are seen as developmentally healthy, resistance melts, and new sources of energy are mobilized for coping with difficult periods.

The article by Ogburn-Colangelo presents a tapescript of actual counseling sessions with a gifted adolescent experiencing conflict between her need to develop her own special abilities and her attachment to family members who do not support the development of these talents. The strategies the counselor used to foster personal growth in the student were *supporting* and *reframing*.

> To support is to validate existing behaviors, attitudes, and emotions. ...To reframe is to assign a new meaning to existing behaviors, attitudes, and emotions—to help the client understand aspects of herself differently, namely, in terms of the process of development. The theory details which behaviors, attitudes, and emotions to reframe and provides both the rationale for the reframing and the framework into which the behavior is placed. (Ogburn-Colangelo, 1979, p. 169)

In this particular case, the counselor validated the student for the strength of her attachment—her ability to experience relationship. At the same time, she invited the young woman to look within herself to discover her own internal pressures toward self-actualization. The counselor helped the student recognize that these two needs might present conflict, and that the conflict was healthy, since both desires were healthy. She also helped the student to acknowledge her strengths: her sense of responsibility to her family, her awareness of her own talents, and her willingness to determine her own future. While encouraging the young woman to trust her own judgment, the counselor at no time demeaned the negative consequences the student might face by following her own path instead of the one designed by her parents.

The counselor was able to see the problem from the student's point of view, and the difficulty of the choices to be made. She listened, helped the student sort out the problem by herself, and gave her confidence in her strengths and her ability to cope with the situation.

> So, in counseling Sara we want to act as nourishers, not so much of the talent itself, but of the emotional structure from which the talent comes. We can accomplish this by supporting and reframing already existing strengths which might stimulate the client to continue that growth (Ogburn-Colangelo, 1979, p. 186).

Unfortunately, few gifted children have the opportunity to discuss their inner conflicts with an experienced counselor. In many cases, their closest contact with a "nourisher" is the specialist who works with gifted children. *All* personnel working with the gifted must be prepared to act in a counseling capacity. Special training in counseling the gifted should be a mandatory part of every training program in gifted education. However, as the state of the art now stands, these abilities are not highly valued by either teachers or teacher-trainers. Hultgren (1981) found that out of a list of 24 teacher competencies in gifted education, counseling was ranked as 14th in importance by both practitioners and university personnel.

We have only begun to explore the emotional development of the gifted. We know that gifted children are highly sensitive, and that this sensitivity must be nurtured in order to develop the child's emotional health. We also know that the level of sensitivity shown by the gifted child is not highly valued in the society. If ever there was a good reason for gifted programs, it would be to provide a safe haven for the emotional development of these children. If we fail to provide the kind of understanding which they so desperately need, we transform emotional sensitivity into emotional disturbance, and we risk losing our most morally advanced individuals. This is a risk none of us can afford to take.

Torn asunder by compelling forces
Buffeted by demands and desires
Encouraged and discouraged all at once
Satisfied, yet left feeling empty
Stretched to the limit and then stretched some more
Grab a breath before being pushed under again

"Wait," "Stop," "No," I scream from the ragged insides
  of my mind.
Who is in charge?
Why is it this way?
I think I am making choices,
But is this what I really thought I wanted?

A cry in the darkness,
A sigh in the space next to me
The world outside my window
The beat of my own heart in the dawning light.

What will this day bring?
How can I gain control?

July, 1979
(A gifted adult)

REFERENCES

Boring, E. G. *A history of experimental psychology* (2nd ed.). Englewood Cliffs NJ: Prentice-Hall, 1950.

Colangelo, N., & Zaffrann, R. T. *New voices in counseling the gifted.* Dubuque IA: Kendall/Hunt, 1979.

Dabrowski, K. Types of increased psychic excitability (in Polish). *Biuletyn Instytutu Higieny Psychizcnej*, 1938, *1*(3–4), 3–26.

Dabrowski, K. *Psychoneurosis is not an illness.* London: Gryf, 1972.

Dabrowski, K., & Piechowski, M. M. *Theory of levels of emotional development* (2 volumes). Oceanside NY: Dabor, 1977.

Dirks, J. Parent's reactions to identification of the gifted. *Roeper Review*, 1979, *2*, 9–10.

Elgersma, R. Providing for affective growth in gifted education. *Roeper Review*, 1981, *3*, 6–7.

Gowan, J. C. Personal communication, April 29, 1982.

Greene, L. A. *Dabrowski's Theory of Emotional Development and Loevinger's Theory of Ego Development: A direct comparison.* Unpublished master's thesis, Northwestern University, 1982.

Hollingworth, L. M. *Children above 180 I.Q., Stanford-Binet.* Yonkers-on-Hudson NY: World Book, 1942.

Hultgren, H. M. *Competencies for teachers of the gifted.* Unpublished doctoral dissertation, University of Denver, June, 1981.

Kohlberg, L. Continuities in childhood and adult moral development revisited. In P. Baltes & K. Schaie, (Eds.), *Life-span developmental psychology.* New York: Academic Press, 1973.

Kohlberg, L. The cognitive-developmental approach to moral education. *Phi Delta Kappan,* 1975, *56,* 670–678.

Kretschmer, E. *[The psychology of men of genius.]* (R. B. Cattell, trans.). New York: Harcourt, Brace, 1931.

Lewis, W. D. Some characteristics of very superior children. *Journal of Genetic Psychology,* 1943, *62,* 301–309.

Lombroso, C. *The man of genius.* London: Robert Scott, 1891.

Marland, S., Jr. *Education of the gifted and talented.* Report to the Congress of the United States by the U.S. Commissioner of Education. Washington DC: U.S. Government Printing Office, March, 1972.

Mehrens, W. A., & Lehman, I. J. *Measurement and evaluation in education and psychology.* New York: Holt, Rinehart & Winston, 1973.

Nisbet, J. F. *The insanity of genius.* London: Kegan Paul, Trench, Trubner & Co., Ltd., 1891.

Ogburn-Colangelo, M. K. Giftedness as multilevel potential: A clinical example. In N. Colangelo & R. T. Zaffrann (Eds.), *New voices in counseling the gifted.* Dubuque IA: Kendall/Hunt, 1979.

Piechowski, M. M. Developmental potential. In N. Colangelo & R. T. Zaffrann (Eds.), *New voices in counseling the gifted.* Dubuque IA: Kendall/Hunt, 1979.

Piechowski, M. M., & Colangelo, N. Profiles of overexcitabilities of gifted adolescents (in preparation).

Piechowski, M. M., Silverman, L. K., Cunningham K., & Falk, R. F. *A comparison of intellectually gifted and artists on five dimensions of mental functioning.* Paper presented at the American Educational Research Association Annual Meeting, New York, March, 1982.

Sanborn, M. P. Counseling the guidance needs of the gifted and talented. In A. H. Passow (Ed.), *The gifted and the talented.* The 78th yearbook of the National Society for the Study of Education. Chicago: University of Chicago Press, 1979.

Silverman, L. K. *Emotional development of gifted children.* Presentation at the Workshop on Counseling, Area I—South Service Center for Gifted Education, Chicago, Illinois, March, 1982.

Silverman, L. K., & Ellsworth, B. The Theory of Positive Disintegration and its implications for giftedness. *Proceedings of the Third International Conference on the Theory of Positive Disintegration.* University of Miami School of Medicine, November, 1980.

Tannenbaum, A. J. Presentation as part of the course, "The nature of intelligence." University of Denver, Denver, Colorado, July, 1982.

Terman, L. M. (Ed.). *Mental and physical traits of a thousand gifted children. Genetic studies of genius* (Vol. 1). Stanford: Stanford University Press, 1925.

Terman, L. M., et al. *Genetic studies of genius* (5 vols.). Stanford: Stanford University Press, 1925–1959.

Terman, L. M., & Oden, M. H. *The gifted child grows up. Genetic studies of genius* (Vol. 4). Stanford: Stanford University Press, 1947.

Treffinger, D. J., Borgers, S. B., Render, G. F., & Hoffman, R. M. Encouraging the affective development: A compendium of techniques and resources. *The Gifted Child Quarterly,* 1976, *20,* 47–65.

Witty, P. A study of one hundred gifted children. *University of Kansas Bulletin of Education,* 1930, *2*(7).

Zaffrann, R. T., & Colangelo, N. Counseling with gifted and talented students. *The Gifted Child Quarterly,* 1977, *21,* 305–321.

CHAPTER FOUR

Who Should Counsel the Gifted: The Role of Educational Personnel

Beverly Ness Parke

If you have spent more than a passing moment with gifted children you already know the answer to the question, "Who can counsel the gifted?" Everyone associated with the gifted serves a counseling function of one type or another. By virtue of the association, the function one serves may vary from adviser to facilitator to listener to advocate. But the overall response is clear; there is a role for many people in the counseling of gifted and talented children and youth.

The world of the gifted child encompasses a constellation of factors including people, concerns, beliefs, and activities. The dynamics of that constellation result in the unique experiences of each individual. For some the interactions are favorable and little or no counseling is sought or needed. Yet for many a less fortunate child, alignment may occur with confusion, uncertainty, or anxiety the end products. In such cases, counseling intervention ranging from minimal to extensive may be needed. As the constellation is fluid, the interactions are constantly changing and so too are individual needs. When dealing with the counseling needs of the gifted, it is imperative to be aware of the ever-changing nature of the individuals, the dynamics of their lives, and the potential for many different people to productively function in the processes of counseling.

Within the context of this discussion, the counseling roles of three educationally related groups will be discussed: teachers, administrators, and pupil personnel staff members. While these roles reflect school-based personnel, the optimum situation involves a joint counseling effort between home and school. Clearly, parents and family members have critical roles to play in the everyday guidance of these students. Dettman and Colangelo (1980) discuss the need for a "partnership approach" to counseling which involves persons from school and home working together to make joint decisions about the needs of gifted students. Both institutions play large roles in development, and they can best benefit the students by doing so in a cooperative manner.

ROLE OF THE TEACHER IN COUNSELING

The counseling roles served by teachers of gifted students are many. In their daily encounters with these students, teachers find themselves fulfilling numerous counseling functions as they attempt to guide the students through their educational careers with as few problems as possible. Teachers must be well informed about the psychosocial needs of the gifted and should use their knowledge of individual students in concert with this more technical information on gifted children as a whole, in order to respond to these needs quickly and appropriately. Among the roles played by teachers are those discussed below.

Advocate/Ombudsperson

The teacher is in a unique position to be the advocate or ombudsperson for gifted students. As teachers are integrally involved with most facets of the students' educational interactions, they are able to represent the students' interests and assist them in a multitude of ways. Teachers can promote programs, talk with parents and administrators about special needs, inform others about giftedness and students' individual needs. As "troubleshooters," teachers can help mold a system which is flexible enough to accommodate individuals with unique educational and psychological needs.

Consultant

Dettman and Colangelo (1980) state that working with parents is an "important factor in the educational development of gifted youngsters" (p. 161). Teachers have contact with parents when they pick up their children after school, come to parent conferences, engage in telephone conversations, and attend special programs during the course of the school year. These opportunities, along with requests for individual consultations, provide teachers with a chance to respond to parental questions and needs regarding their gifted children. Forming alliances with parents can help define a consistent approach to educational experiences both at home and at school. Teachers must feel free to consult with parents in order to make these alliances possible.

The teacher may also play a key role in counseling gifted children by consulting with other educational personnel. By being available to discuss individual students with other teachers, administrators, counselors, psychologists, or social workers, the teacher can acquaint them with the needs of gifted children and provide information which may be helpful in gaining their understanding and support in providing appropriate programming and educational support.

Diagnostician

While teachers do not play the primary role in psychological assessment, they do observe students, talk with parents and other teachers, and do some academic testing. Thus, teachers have a great deal of diagnostic-type information on students' psychological and academic performance levels. It may be the teacher who first notices a student's academic potential, possible psychological problems, or inability to see the chalkboard, for example. As observer/diagnostician, the teacher can make preliminary judgments and refer the student, as necessary, to the proper person for further assessment.

As diagnostician for classroom purposes, the teacher can provide an important service by assessing current skill levels and providing materials and curricular options which are at the child's achievement levels. Many of the problems associated with giftedness (e.g., boredom, underachievement) may thus be avoided, averting potential future problems.

Listener

One of the most critical roles a teacher can play in the counseling of gifted students is that of listener. It is not unusual for gifted children to need someone to talk to about problems, ideas, encounters, or just life in general. Being a listener involves attending to the students and allowing them to speak freely about the topics they wish to discuss. Just having a nonjudgmental and nonthreatening outlet for their thoughts can be a useful resource for the gifted.

Adviser

As an adviser, the teacher might offer suggestions to the gifted students on a wide range of subjects when asked. These could include possible colleges to apply to, whom to see in order to attend special art classes, what books to read in order to learn more about the Phoenicians, or how to get along with other students in the class. When serving as an adviser, the teacher must use professional judgment in deciding when it is appropriate to initiate suggestions and when students are best left to their own devices.

Instructor

To complement the advisory role, the teacher can also serve an important counseling function by instructing students in methods of dealing with such matters as problem solving, interpersonal relationships, and values. By so doing, the classroom teacher can help students to know more about themselves and can assist them in their interactions by teaching methods to facilitate those processes. Teaching students to help themselves in this manner provides them with the skills to function apart from the school and leads them to the capability of functioning as mature responsible persons.

Facilitator

There may come a time when advising and instructing is not sufficient and direct intervention is necessary to regain individual or group equilibrium. At such a time, alternative procedures such as group counseling techniques (Allan & Fox, 1979) may be necessary. If the teacher is unable to cope with the individual or group needs, the counseling staff should be asked for assistance. However, the teacher can do some counseling in the classroom.

In addition, the teacher can facilitate students' progress by insuring that individual learning needs are recognized and that curricular options are offered. Mentors, special classes, and individual projects are among the options for providing the differentiated curriculum necessary for gifted students.

Role Model

Teachers must be aware that they can effect positive growth in their students by modeling the behaviors they wish students to exhibit. If teachers display tolerance of individual differences, patience with others, and appreciation of excellence, students may begin to recognize such attributes as admirable and begin to display them, too. Students in daily contact with teachers who have a zest for learning, curiosity, a sense of humor, and appreciation for the rights of others may well find themselves wanting to make those attributes their own.

ROLE OF THE ADMINISTRATOR IN COUNSELING

School administrators, be they superintendents, principals, or central administrative staff members, also have key roles in counseling gifted students. As primary decision makers, they are able to effect both personal and institutional changes needed to ensure that these students have the educational and support services they need to flourish in the school setting. In addition, administrators' personal contact with students and their parents is important. Many of the counseling roles filled by administrators are described in what follows.

Advocate

First and foremost, administrators must serve as institutional advocates for these students. This involves keeping the interests of the gifted in mind when making decisions regarding program and curriculum, and being willing to build flexibility into school programming schedules, allowing students to assemble programs responsive to their individual needs. Administrators must also be certain that appropriate educational opportunities are available for students to take advantage of throughout their enrollment. Among the options are special classes, early entrance to school (Alexander & Skinner, 1980), special schools, and activities outside the school such as mentorships and university classes.

Consultant

Like the teacher, the administrator is often called upon to play a consulting role within the district, with parents, and with community members. Within the district, administrators should ensure that teachers and other personnel have received some training regarding gifted students. This may be in the form of classes or professional development activities. By seeing to it that staff is trained, administrators help to ensure higher quality programming.

Consulting with parents and community members regarding the gifted usually takes the form of outlining program options and other district-sponsored programs available to students. While outlining these options, administrators can serve an instructional role by informing their constituents of the district's capabilities and plans for further expansion of programs. At the same time, administrators should attempt to solicit support for current and future programming efforts.

Program Leader

In the position of program leader, the administrator plays a counseling role by making sure that programming options are in place, that counseling capabilities are available, and that excellence is paramount. When programs are in place, the administrator should take steps to see that they run smoothly and continuously. It can be very disruptive to students' progress to lose such programs midway through their schooling.

Listener/Adviser

Gifted students will approach administrators for counsel in personal and academic matters, as they do teachers. It is essential that administrators take time to listen and respond. This may mean making an appointment or just taking a focused moment in the hallway. Attending to the personal needs of students should not be beyond the scope of administrators' counseling roles.

ROLE OF THE PUPIL PERSONNEL STAFF IN COUNSELING

The part played by pupil personnel staff in counseling the gifted combines many of the roles described for teachers and administrators with functions that are uniquely their own. While serving as *advocates* for the gifted in the personal and institutional manners described above, pupil personnel staff can also serve as advocates for special groups within the gifted population such as the culturally diverse (Colangelo & Lafrenz, 1981), the handicapped, and female gifted students. Because these groups have unique needs, their situations should be represented and accounted for. The pupil personnel staff also fills a *consulting* role in dealing with teachers, parents, and administrators. This function, outlined in depth by Zaffrann (1978), may involve acquainting these groups with the nature of giftedness, programming options, or counseling techniques they can use in their daily associations with students. However, the role of this staff does involve certain additional specialized activities which are outlined below.

Diagnostician

While teachers do serve a role in diagnostics, the pupil personnel staff takes primary responsibility for responding to assessment needs of gifted students. These involve assessing for screening and identification for programs, assessing for possible early entrance to school, and assessing identified problems. These problems could be associated with underachievement, behavior problems, or physical disabilities, for example. The pupil personnel staff responds by assessing students and recommending special provisions or additional testing.

Instructor

Some students may need regular counseling in order to begin to handle their environment in a healthy and productive manner. In such cases, pupil personnel staff members may be able to instruct students in coping techniques. These may be in individual or group sessions, depending on which is most appropriate. Staff members can also serve a more preventive function by becoming involved routinely with gifted students as an integral part of gifted programming. By working with students regularly, staff members may be able to prevent the occurrence of serious problems.

Listener/Adviser

The "open door" policy of many counselors is designed to encourage students to come and talk as they feel it is necessary. Counselors trained as listeners can serve as independent and objective third parties for students' concerns or as "safety valves" in matters of crisis intervention. As adviser to these students, the counselor can also assist in problem solving. However, the advisory role extends far beyond those boundaries.

As advisers, pupil personnel staff members should enter into the discussion of such matters as career goals, vocational choices, university admissions procedures, and scholarship availability. These areas are essential to many gifted students and should be handled in a manner which recognizes their importance. Career and vocational guidance should continue throughout a student's education. Information on institutes of higher education and financial aid becomes increasingly necessary as students enter and progress through secondary schools. Accurate, up-to-date information available at the appropriate time can make a critical difference in the educational growth of gifted students.

Liaison to Community Services

It is becoming increasingly unrealistic to assume that all the needs of gifted students can be accommodated by the schools. With decreasing enrollments and increasing costs, schools are being forced to look to the community for educational support. The pupil personnel staff can coordinate this effort for the gifted by serving as liaisons to other institutions providing educational experiences. These might include museums, colleges and universities, science centers, and businesses. The classes can work to assure that students will receive credit for experiences and classes outside the school and can cultivate the opportunities so they are available and profitable for the students involved.

CONCLUSION

Many people throughout the educational system serve counseling roles in the guidance of the gifted—teachers, administrators, and members of the pupil personnel staff have been discussed here. Counseling can assist gifted students in meeting their potentials, coping with their problems, and planning their futures. It is the responsibility of school districts to make sure that such services are available and that personnel are trained to recognize and respond to the needs of their gifted students.

REFERENCES

Alexander, P., & Skinner, M. The effects of early entrance on subsequent social and academic development: A follow-up study. *Journal for the Education of the Gifted*, 1980, 3(3), 147–150.

Allan, S., & Fox, D. Group counseling the gifted. *Journal for the Education of the Gifted,* 1979, *3*(2), 83–92.

Colangelo, N., & Lafrenz, N. Counseling the culturally diverse gifted. *Gifted Child Quarterly,* 1981, *25*(1), 27–30.

Dettmann, D., & Colangelo, N. A functional model for counseling parents of gifted students. *Gifted Child Quarterly,* 1980, *24*(4) 158–161.

Jordan, J., & Keith, J. The counselor's role in working with gifted. In J. Gowan & E. Torrance (Eds.), *Educating the ablest.* Itasca IL: F. E. Peacock, 1971.

Zaffrann, R. Gifted and talented students: Implications for school counselors. *Roeper Review,* 1978, *1*(2), 9–13.

CHAPTER FIVE

Collaboration of Teachers and Counselors in Serving Affective Needs of Gifted Students

Joyce VanTassel-Baska

Many educators question the need for special counseling services for gifted students, some on the grounds that in general, they need no special services and others on the grounds that such services should be sought outside school—through private sources or parents themselves. As in so many other areas of social need, however, the schools must take responsibility for the total education and guidance of children with whom they are entrusted, including the gifted. To do less is to jeopardize the healthy development of children whose parents cannot afford outside counseling assistance.

If public schools are to make a contribution in this area, two key groups need to collaborate—teachers of the gifted and school counselors. Currently, few models exist of programs where responsibility is being shared. Yet the limitations of personnel and time dictate a need for staff collaboration to provide appropriate services.

RATIONALE FOR DIFFERENTIAL COUNSELING

Much of the work in education of the gifted has focused un differential characteristics and needs of the population. Affective and cognitive differences become focal points for creating special counseling interventions which have been viewed as critical in three specific areas: psychosocial, academic, and career/life planning (see Chapter 4). Table 1 (VanTassel-Baska, 1989) depicts the relationship between characteristics of a gifted population and the counseling approach necessary to address them.

Table 1. Relationship between characteristics of gifted students and counseling approaches.

Characteristics	Counseling Provision
Cluster 1 • ability to manipulate abstract symbol systems • retention rate • quickness in learning and mastering the environment	Academic program planning that matches learner cognitive needs
Cluster 2 • ability to do many things well (multipotentiality) • varied and diverse interests • internal locus of control (independence)	Life/career planning that presents atypical models
Cluster 3 • heightened sensitivity • sense of justice • perfectionism	Psychosocial counseling that focuses on the preservation of affective differences

In their comprehensive summary of the literature on the psychosocial characteristics of gifted children, Janos and Robinson (1985) concluded that gifted children as a group possess more positive personal-social characteristics than their nongifted peers. Nevertheless, an individual gifted child who manifests the characteristics listed in Table 1 to an intense degree may suffer in various ways without appropriate counseling intervention. The nature of such suffering could manifest itself in (a) social isolation, either self-imposed or brought about by peer ostracism; (b) social accommodation, by creating a reversal or homogenization of the gifted characteristics, or (c) social acceptance-seeking by denying that the giftedness exists and finding ways to diminish its influence. Any of these conditions may be deleterious for a gifted child. Special counseling is needed that extends well beyond that required for a more typical learner.

In our society, systematic exploration of feelings is limited to two areas of study: (a) literature and the arts and (b) various forms of psychotherapy. It is little wonder then that gifted students lack counseling support, particularly as it relates to feelings about themselves, others, and the world around them. Some educators have argued that affective needs of gifted students mirror those of more typical children. On the other hand, differential affective characteristics have been attributed to the gifted (Clark, 1988; Piechowski, 1979; Silverman, 1983, 1986) and do, in my opinion, exist. Table 2 presents a synthesis of five key social-emotional needs of gifted students that differ phenomenologically from those of more typical students. A strategy for addressing each of the five is also included for counselors and teachers to consider.

Reasons for counseling the gifted as a specific group are embedded within their psychological make-up and manifested as special needs in the context of a school environment. The use of key school personnel to develop systematic interventions is a necessary part of building an effective school counseling program for these students.

ROLE OF SCHOOL COUNSELORS

We may realistically expect school counselors to provide some counseling to the gifted. It is unrealistic, however, to expect them to make this a major focus of their work, as a counselor load in most school systems ranges from 300–500 students. Working with gifted students under such circumstances may be perceived as simply an added responsibility. Another deterrent to needed

Table 2. Social-emotional needs of gifted students.

Social-Emotional Need	Strategies for Addressing Needs
• To understand ways in which they are different from other children and ways in which they are the same	• Use bibliotherapy techniques • Establish group discussions • Hold individual dialogue sessions
• To appreciate and treasure their own individuality and the individual differences of others	• Promote biography study • Honor diverse talents through awards, performance sessions, special seminars, and symposia • Encourage contest and competitive entry
• To understand and develop social skills that allow them to cope adequately within relationships	• Do creative problem solving in dyads and small groups • Create role-playing scenarios • Devise appropriate simulation activities
• To develop an appreciation for their high-level sensitivity that manifests itself in humor, artistic endeavors, and intensified emotional experiences	• Encourage positive and expressive outlets for sensitivity such as tutoring, volunteer work, art, music, and drama • Promote journal writing that captures feelings about key experiences
• To gain a realistic assessment of their abilities and talents and how they can be nurtured • To develop an understanding of the distinction between "pursuit of excellence" and "pursuit of perfection"	• Provide for regular assessment procedures • Provide for grouping opportunities with others of similar abilities and interests • Create a "safe" environment to experiment with failure • Promote risk-taking behavior
• To learn the art and science of compromise	• Provide "cooperation games" • Work on goal setting • Encourage the development of a philosophy of life

Note: From "Counseling the Gifted" by Joyce VanTassel-Baska in J. Feldhusen, J. VanTassel-Baska, & K. Seeley, *Excellence in Educating the Gifted,* 1989, Denver, CO: Love Publishing.

counseling services is the lack of counselors in elementary schools. In these settings, only teachers and occasionally a principal are available to perform the needed functions. The major problem, however, relates to a lack of understanding of the nature of counseling needed by gifted students.

Some general strategies that counselors could use to help meet social-emotional needs of gifted students might include the following:

1. The establishment of a counseling consortium within a school district or across districts, made up of mental health specialists in the community, social workers, psychologists, and counselors. Such a consortium would be available to individual students and families as needed on a case basis. A hotline might be established for purposes of crisis intervention.
2. The establishment of parent education services that focus on the socio-emotional and related counseling needs of their children. Speakers, group discussion, and case-study problem solving comprise three viable approaches to organizing such efforts. Purely informational sessions could be included with problem-solving sessions.
3. The establishment of student counseling seminars that deal with gifted students in a group context. Organized and run by a designated teacher or counselor, such sessions can be planned at least monthly to focus on the specific needs delineated earlier in this chapter. Using gifted students in the planning and implementation of such seminars heightens their effectiveness.
4. The establishment of inservice seminars for regular classroom teachers that offer information on the nature of giftedness, the cognitive and affective needs of different kinds of gifted learners, and discussion of strategies for meeting these needs within the framework of the regular classroom.

Typically, the role of the counselor at middle school and high school levels has deteriorated to performing routine functions such as scheduling, attendance, and follow-up referral cases, usually of truancy, maladaptive classroom behavior, and substance abuse. Thus the classical definition of a counselor as "one who guides" has been replaced by "one who responds to institutional demands."

School counselors may derive great satisfaction in helping gifted learners maximize their potential abilities. Within the limits of the situation that currently exists in most schools, counselors will probably be most successful in their efforts on behalf of gifted children by working with groups of children, parents, classroom teachers, and teachers who provide supplementary or replacement types of special education to gifted learners.

SPECIFIC TEACHER STRATEGIES FOR COUNSELING

While the school counselor can perform many valuable services for the gifted, the classroom teacher also has an important counseling function because many problems of the gifted first surface and need attention in daily contact with peers.

In the psychosocial domain, teachers are in an excellent position to provide guidance to gifted students in several areas of general concern. These guidance techniques may be seen as integral to other teaching and learning activities that are taking place in the classroom. They may be used profitably by regular classroom teachers and teachers of the gifted.

Reading books that have a gifted child as protagonist can help students identify some of their problems in others. Thus through discussion gifted students can come to a new awareness about how to cope with such problems.

For example, *Lord of the Flies,* by William Golding, can help students understand differences among individuals. Key questions to ask about the book include:

- Why was Piggy ostracized by the group?
- What might he have done to prevent such treatment?
- What happens to people who feel rejected, according to the author?
- Can you think of a time when you have felt rejected? How did you respond or react? How might you have changed your behavior to obtain more favorable results?

An excellent teacher reference for this type of activity is a booklist from the National Council of Teachers of English entitled *The Gifted Child in Literature* (Tway, 1980).

Educational therapy techniques can provide approaches to address socio-emotional issues. Bibliotherapy, biography, journal writing, and art all can serve dual purposes. They are valid curricular devices within programs for the gifted, but they are carefully structured to provide a context for students to discuss feelings, as well as ideas. Instructional strategies necessary to fulfill this purpose include discussion and debriefing after students have read, viewed, or heard particular presentations of material. Careful Socratic questioning can draw attention to feelings evoked by the materials leading students to a deeper understanding of their own and others' feelings. More structured literature-based programs such as Junior Great Books and Philosophy for Children also have potential for adoption in these areas.

A second area of psychosocial development that teachers can help gifted students explore is their sense of perfectionism. By focusing on open-ended activities and leading students to engage in "safe" risk-taking behaviors, teachers can establish a climate that encourages students to realize that most situations in life do not require *one* right answer. An example of such an activity follows.

Pass out pictures (one for every three students) that are impressionistic in style, and ask students to respond to these stimuli according to the following paradigm:

1. What do you observe in the picture? (Make a list of what you see.)
2. What ideas does your picture convey?
3. What feelings does your picture evoke?
4. If you were to identify with an object in your picture, what would you identify with and why?
5. Now spend a few minutes synthesizing your observations, ideas, feelings, and reactions to the picture in whatever form you wish. You may choose to write a poem, draw a picture, create a descriptive story, etc.

After each student has responded individually to these questions and activities, have groups of three discuss each other's perceptions of the pictures. The instructor then may ask individual students to share their pictures and their reactions to them. Follow-up may include whole-group discussion of similarities and differences among the pictures. Such an activity can also introduce a unit of study on cultural or individual differences.

A third area of exploration with gifted students is forming meaningful relationships and developing friendships. For this area of psychosocial development, the use of bibliotherapy techniques may be the most useful. Books such as *The Bunny Who Wanted a Friend* (Berg, 1966), suitable for primary age students, is a good example of a key tool. Questions like the following can be used to elicit understanding of the strategies by which we gain friends:

1. What are all the reasons that the bunny did not have a friend?
2. What was wrong with his method of making friends?
3. What was his "secret" to finally finding a friend?
4. What if you were a bunny? How would you have tried to get a friend?

5. Why were the bunny and the bird friends at the end of the story? List all the reasons.

Teachers can also develop units that focus on some of these key topics. A sample list of possible unit topics follows:

- Understanding others
- Tolerance
- Coping with being gifted
- Sensitivity
- Positive uses of humor
- Forming relationships

Each unit should include various reading material that focuses on the topic, lists of discussion questions to be used with gifted students in small groups, and possible follow-up projects.

CAREER EXPLORATION

The suggestions presented in this section can be implemented by counselors and teachers. Teachers can incorporate these areas into their teaching and focus on them with gifted students. Writing experiences and questioning strategies, in particular, are relatively easy modifications to make that can have a great impact on students.

By the fifth and sixth grades, gifted students need assistance with academic planning, thinking through ideas they have about careers, and pursuing areas of interest. Again the role of teachers is critical in shaping appropriate options. According to a memo from prestigious colleges to secondary school principals, parents, and students, there are several areas of concern regarding the lack of preparation for college of bright students. These areas include:

- Reading at an analytical and interpretative level
- Writing essays
- Solid "discipline study"
- Essay exam opportunities
- Critical thought and inquiry

Academic advising implies knowing what preparation colleges recommend for students. Background in a foreign language, for example, is a key ingredient in a talented student's profile, yet many counseling departments ignore its importance in building programs for talented learners. The following basic program constitutes a strong academic preparation for talented learners, according to the Consortium for the Advancement of Higher Education (CAHE):

- English (3 years)
- Mathematics (3 years)
- History (2 years)
- Science (1 year of lab science)
- Foreign language (3 years of one language)
- Arts (study of art, music, drama, dance)

Exposure to atypical career models is another area of need for the gifted. Silverman (1983) has generated some key prototypes that are worthy of discussion in the classroom:

- Delaying decision making
- Having serial or concurrent careers
- Pursuing interests as avocations
- Keeping multiple options
- Synthesizing interests from many fields
- Exploring real-life experiences
- Creating new or unusual careers
- Exploring life themes for career choice

One example from this list, delaying decision making, is important for gifted students to practice. Knowing that many important individuals in various fields did not make career decisions until the end of their undergraduate experience can be meaningful information to students struggling to make a career decision early. The following activities can be used by teachers to help such students grapple with the issues:

1. Read biographies of five important people in fields you are interested in. Track the development of their careers in terms of the issue of "timing."
2. Interview someone in your area(s) of interest. Research their early decision-making patterns.
3. "Shadow" a professional in a field of interest. Analyze the most important skills they have and relate them to the educational background they received. What is the correlation?

4. Survey a group of recent college graduates from your geographical area. Include questions related to when they decided on a career direction and whether they are still pursuing that direction. Report your results.

Each of the other career prototype issues for the gifted can be similarly explored by teachers structuring appropriate activities.

VanTassel-Baska (1981) outlined a series of six strands for teachers and counselors to focus on in career planning for gifted students. These strands from kindergarten to Grade 12 highlight the following areas:
1. Biography reading and discussion.
2. Small group counseling on special issues and concerns (e.g., group dynamics, life planning, coping).
3. Mentor models and independent study.
4. Individual assessment of abilities, interests, and personality attributes.
5. Academic preparation for high school and college career exploration.
6. Internship opportunities.

This scope and sequence of key elements in a gifted and talented career counseling program provide emphasis on the psychosocial needs and the need for planning and decision making among the gifted population.

A PARTNERSHIP: COUNSELORS AND TEACHERS

Since school counselors, regular classroom teachers, and parents are often either unavailable or unskilled in counseling gifted students, one viable delivery system alternative for providing guidance to the gifted is the teacher of the gifted. In many settings, these individuals work with gifted children for varying amounts of time in the popular "pull-out" delivery system, and see the behavior of the gifted child from an objective stance and on an ongoing basis. They also have access to groups of gifted students at a given time. Frequently, these teachers are also knowledgeable about the nature and needs of gifted children, both cognitive and affective. Thus the teacher of the gifted may be in the best position to provide the guidance so needed by the gifted student who generally spends most of his or her time in the regular classroom.

Teachers of the gifted present a reasonable alternative to meeting many counseling needs. A segment of time each week could be set aside to attend to specific issues as well as when they arise in the classroom—for example, frustration at a less than perfect paper; disappointment about peers' lack of enthusiasm for a shared project; feelings of rejection at not being selected as the "best" student. Teachers of the gifted can frequently diagnose and effectively remedy such problems. In many instances such teacher interventions are quite successful.

Ideally, regular classroom teachers could provide fully for the special cognitive and affective needs of gifted children in their classrooms. This is not impossible in the light of advanced concepts of differentiation of curriculum and individualization of teaching materials and methods. We should certainly work continually toward that goal. On the other hand, it is unlikely to occur on a large scale in the immediate future. Accordingly, we shall conclude this chapter with a discussion of what may be perhaps the most realistic compromise to consider in implementing counseling programs for the gifted, that is, a partnership of school counselors and teachers of the gifted. The following list depicts the strengths of each partner.

School Counselors

- Trained in general counseling and guidance techniques.
- Sensitive to affective issues at various development stages.
- Available to arrange mentorships, internships, special programs.
- Trained to administer and interpret special tests and inventories.
- Familiar with role-modeling techniques.
- Capable of diagnosing problem areas in students' psychosocial development.

Teachers of the Gifted

- Trained in effective intervention techniques with gifted learners.
- Sensitive to affective issues.
- Available to handle psychosocial issues on a daily basis in the classroom.
- Trained to translate assessment information into program options.

- Familiar with key gifted individuals who could serve as role models.
- Capable of prescribing classroom activities that could assist in positive psychosocial development.

Each role is critical to implementing a successful counseling program. A good general background in counseling and guidance provides a workable framework. Understanding the positive deviances of a gifted population provides the specific translation needed to make such programs effective. Responsibility for the overall counseling program then might be divided according to the following job description.

Counselor for the Gifted (10% Time)

1. Work with individual cases as referred.
2. Provide small-group counseling sessions across grade levels once every 2 weeks (1 hour each).
3. Establish mentorship-internship directories.
4. Develop a monthly lecture/discussion series on key career areas of interest to gifted students.
5. Sponsor a high school trip to selected colleges and universities for gifted/talented students.
6. Hold semi-annual planning sessions for parents of the gifted.

Teacher of the Gifted (10% of Instructional Time)

1. Provide activities that promote positive psychosocial development among the gifted.
2. Implement an effective curriculum that focuses on the needs of the gifted.
3. Provide speakers in the classroom who are good role models for the gifted.
4. Prepare bibliographies that focus on the best of biography and autobiography and/or in fiction that focus on a gifted student as a protagonist.
5. Utilize small-group and individual consultation as strategies to promote social and self-understanding.
6. Use literature and art as tools to blend cognitive and affective issues.

In this way, the responsibility is shared for meeting the counseling needs of the gifted, and the task does not become overwhelming to either counselors or teachers.

CONCLUSION

Most of the strategies suggested are highly cost effective but do require reorganizing instructional time and differential staffing of pupil services personnel. Such administrative changes may be met with initial resistance, but over time can and do prove themselves effective. Staff training coupled with the development of counseling curriculum units can help solidify the ideas and techniques. (The Appendix provides such a unit developed by a school counselor for use at the elementary level.) It is also important to note that these strategies should not be viewed as isolated alternatives but rather as interrelated parts of a comprehensive counseling program for the gifted.

There are many problems associated with counseling the gifted in school settings. Since it is unlikely that schools can be easily changed, it behooves gifted educators to find workable approaches that accommodate the current structure of schools and recognize the nature of the constraints within the structure. Modifying and adapting current practice is always easier than instituting a new job. Thus teachers and counselors can cooperatively structure new opportunities for affective growth of gifted students, secure in the knowledge that such a program can be implemented without major trauma.

REFERENCES

Berg, J. (1966). *The bunny who wanted a friend.* New York: Golden Press.

Clark, B. (1988). *Growing up gifted* (3rd ed.). Columbus, OH: Charles Merrill.

Colangelo, N., & Zaffrann, R. (1979). *New directions in counseling the gifted.* Dubuque, IA: Kendall-Hunt.

Crouse, J. (1979). The effects of academic ability. In C. Jencks et al., *Who gets ahead* (pp. 85–121). New York: Basic Books.

Janos, P., & Robinson, N. (1985). Psychological development in intellectually gifted children. In F. D. Horowitz & M. O'Brien (Eds.), *The gifted and talented: Developmental perspectives* (pp. 149–195). Washington, DC: American Psychological Association.

Piechowski, M. (1979). The developmental potential of the gifted. In N. Colangelo, & R. Zaffrann, *New directions in counseling the gifted.* Dubuque, IA: Kendall Hunt.

Silverman, L. (1983). Personality development: The pursuit of excellence. *Journal for the Education of the Gifted, 6*(1), 5–19.

Silverman, L. (1986). What happens to the gifted girl? In J. Maker (Ed.), *Critical issues in gifted education* (pp. 43–89). Rockville, MD: Aspen Systems.

Tway, E. (1980). The gifted child in literature. *Language Arts, 57*(1), 14–20.

VanTassel-Baska, J. (1981). A comprehensive model of career education for the gifted and talented. *Journal of Career Education, 7*(4), 325–331.

VanTassel-Baska, J. (1989). Counseling the gifted. In J. Feldhusen, J. VanTassel-Baska, & K. Seeley (Eds.), *Excellence in educating the gifted* (pp. 299–314). Denver, CO: Love Publishing.

APPENDIX TO CHAPTER FIVE

A Small Group Counseling Unit for Gifted Elementary Students

Linda Coye

This unit is designed for students in Grades 2–4 but could be extended to fifth and possibly sixth grade. All students can benefit from guidance and counseling units that focus on self-awareness and esteem building, peer and adult relations, and decision-making and problem-solving skills. Those students who have been identified as talented and gifted (TAG) have an additional burden within the affective domain. They face the dichotomy of being different and yet wanting to be "just like everybody else." By second grade the TAG distinction is becoming more apparent to the peer group and acceptance by that group is more important to the TAG child. The purpose of this unit is to provide an arena for TAG students to explore, discuss, and more fully understand the issues and implications of the "gifted" label.

This unit has been designed specifically to meet affective needs of the gifted learner. The generic structures of small group counseling have formed the foundation and framework. The needs and issues of the gifted child have given the unit its unique character. "What does it mean to be gifted?" is a recurring counseling theme. "Getting along" within the institution of the school and with peers and significant adults are two other major topics to be addressed.

A component has been included to allow later sessions to be tailored to the specific issues targeted to particular group needs as perceived by the counselor or students. As in most guidance/counseling situations, developing students' self-esteem is a fundamental underlying objective. It is within a counseling setting that students can experiment and discuss without the impediment of grades.

Evaluation of the unit may be accomplished by including self-reflection and check points through utilizing the journaling process. A major portion of the unit will focus on discussion. Also, peer interaction will be encouraged through cooperative games, activities, and projects. Since a sense of humor is a hallmark of the gifted, students may be encouraged to have a weekly joke or riddle.

Setting. Small group; 8–10 students (cross grade and gender grouping).

Duration. Once a week, 45 minutes per session; 9 weeks or sessions. (This number is flexible to meet the needs of the group and the constraints of school scheduling.)

Instructors. School counselor and teacher of the gifted (team).

Major content outline. Sessions are sequenced as follows:

1. Setting up the group—ground rules, group building, structures. Activity: gripes.
2. What does it mean to be gifted?
3. School is. . . .
4. It's all so boring.
5. Adults! Their care and feeding.
6. Cooperation and competition.
7. What is a friend?
8. More about me: Perfection blues.
9. Celebration and evaluation.

Sample Lesson

1. Journaling and Check-In. As soon as students arrive, have them find a quiet place to write. Journal entries should be personal and reflective. Have students fill out the check-in sheet. Note: This sheet will survey topics of concern and will form the basis for tailoring the group to the students' needs and interests.
2. Discovering people's gifts
   a. Split the group in half and hand out a list of famous persons. Activity directions: Name the person and the gift the person has; emphasize the gift, not the occupation (e.g., the President—leadership, Sandra Day O'Connor—studying, making decisions). Report back and leader makes a group list and clarifies where necessary. (Students should be able to know the person from reputation or a quick look through available library books.)
   b. List lesser known people and their gifts—things they do well, are interested in, or a personal trait and anything special that impressed you (e.g., teacher—patience, parent—building, figuring, etc.).

c. Summarize: What are gifts? What does it mean to be "gifted"?
3. How are "gifts" discovered?
   a. Choose a well-known personality, e.g., Michael Jordan. What are his gifts/abilities?
   b. As a youngster what would you expect to see him doing?
   c. Discussion questions:
      - Do you think Michael Jordan might have felt different at some time?
      - What gifts do you have that the school has discovered?
      - Have you ever felt different?
      - What are other things you enjoy or are interested in?
      - How would you explain "being gifted" to a friend or grandmother?
4. Exploring our gifts—Each of us has gifts. Some of the gifts have been discovered, others we may not find until we're grown up. One clue, however, is that gifts may be things we like to do or are interested in. Choose one of the product alternatives to show the things you like to do, are interested in, or would like to try in the future.
   a. Make a piece of wrapping paper illustrating your interests.
   b. Make a gift box—put pictures or words inside the box and choose a wrapping paper that is you.
   c. Write a poem about yourself.
   d. Write a story about "the gifts."
   e. Role play or puppet play a dialogue between you and a friend about your being gifted.
   f. Write a rap.
   g. Design a collage of your interests and abilities.

CHAPTER SIX

The Parent's Role in Counseling the Gifted: The Balance Between Home and School

Arlene Munger

It is probably obvious to most people that the parent functions, with or without advice from others, as the infant's on-line nutritionist, hygienist, physical therapist, language coach, safety engineer, general educator, and special tutor. Perhaps it is not so obvious, but equally true, that the parent serves as guidance counselor in the development of the child's interests and abilities, personal-social adjustment, affective behaviors, and interpersonal relationships.

The nature and extent of this parent/child counseling relationship which evolves (or fails to evolve) is likely to have a powerful impact on the child's emotional and personal-social development—including the child's ability to seek, accept, and profit from counseling by appropriate others. This is no less true for the average or below average child than for the gifted child. Rather, the role of the parent as counselor for the gifted child varies more in degree than in substance and may be made easier or more difficult according to the unique circumstances involved. In this sense, it is not unlike the role played by parents of children who are physically or mentally impaired.

Factors which may affect the nature of the counseling relationship between the parent and the gifted child include:

1. *The parent's perception of behavioral traits associated with gifted children as positive or negative and the degree to which the child exhibits them.* These include high physical and psychological energy; intense curiosity; a lesser need for sleep; a tendency to question authority; unevenness of development; sensitivity to interpersonal relationships; and increased awareness of feelings.
2. *The degree of match between the parent's abilities and those of the child.* Parents may intuitively understand the child's perceptions and reactions because they had similar experiences as children; or parents may be confused or puzzled because the child's perceptions and reactions appear alien to their own experiences.
3. *The availability of human resources.* The parents of the gifted child may find it more difficult to locate professionals (e.g., pediatricians, counselors, educators) who are familiar with the unique characteristics and needs of gifted children and who can offer counsel. Family members, friends and neighbors may be less supporting of the parents and view the child as an oddity to be either admired or pitied.
4. *The accelerated rate of intellectual development—particularly in relation to emotional and social growth.* Any existing problems tend to be intensified when the child reaches school age. Teachers impressed with the child's knowledge and skill may expect similar maturity in emotional and social areas.
5. *The presence of other siblings in the family who are not perceived as gifted.* Siblings who are less able or not perceived as gifted may resent the gifted child, suffer from feelings of inferiority, or react with anger or aggression. The parents may feel guilty over the differential treatment of the children and attempt to compensate in inappropriate ways.

A paradox for parents of the gifted child is that the more skillful they are in guiding the intellectual, academic, and social growth of the child prior to school entry, the greater dissonance there may be between the child and his or her chronological age peers and the more likely that the youngster will encounter difficulties in school adjustment and peer relationships if differentiated educational opportunities are not available.

The parent as counselor can hope to minimize adverse side effects of the child's accelerated intellectual and social maturity by paying equally close attention to the development of facilitative affective behaviors and skill in interpersonal relationships. The gifted child's increased sensitivity and heightened awareness of feelings can enable him or her to develop empathy and insight which leads to understanding, acceptance, and appreciation of his or her own abilities and those of other children whose interests and skills may differ. The gifted child who feels secure and confident is more likely to find as much or more satisfaction in self-competition as in competition against others and is therefore better able to offer assistance and encouragement to less able peers without being overbearing or obnoxious.

Early parental guidance in the development of leadership skills and understanding of the responsibilities attendent on leaders together with the gifted child's tendency to have a strong sense of fair play and high ethical and moral standards should enable the child to derive satisfaction from heterogeneous relationships without exploiting those who are less able. (To become an effective leader the child should also experience the role of being a good follower.)

TECHNIQUES FOR PARENTS

The following points may be useful for parents to keep in mind as they actively participate in the counseling and guidance role with their gifted child or children. While it can be said that no two gifted children are alike, general principles do seem to apply in this area, particularly when children are young.

1. Be alert to spontaneous expressions of interest in the environment. Provide additional opportunities to acquire knowledge and experience in these areas. Encourage self-initiated exploration of the environment, materials, and activities available while providing sufficient safeguards to prevent injury.
2. Talk to your child as you care for him or her; carry the child about and cuddle him or her. Use your regular vocabulary and talk about what you are doing (e.g., preparing food, bathing, dressing, going for the mail, etc.).
3. Expose the child to music, art objects, and reading. Provide a variety of materials (e.g., classical music as well as nursery rhymes). Note the child's preferences and involve the child in decisions early by offering a choice between or among acceptable alternatives (e.g., the blue or red shirt; a cracker or toast; a bath before or after dinner).
4. Talk about the properties or attributes of objects—color, size, shape, utility, texture, etc.—and encourage the child to note similarities and differences.
5. Be sensitive to the child's moods, degree of well-being (e.g., fatigue, illness, overstimulation, etc.) and allow for lapses in performance levels without being critical.
6. Encourage your child's sense of playfulness and the ridiculous as well as interest in innovation and inventiveness. Select toys that lend themselves to multiple uses but don't underestimate your

child's ability for adapting common toys or objects to uncommon application.
7. Broaden the child's personal, social, physical and learning environment through activities which take into account physical, social, and intellectual development. Don't underestimate his or her ability to profit from activities which might not normally be associated with chronological age. Let the child set the pace. First experiences may need to be largely observational with the degree of active participation increasing as the child's confidence and interest are aroused. As a rule, parental involvement in the form of encouragement, equipment, and special lessons should be geared to the degree of interest the child demonstrates. Encouragement and support of the child's demonstrated interest will nurture the development of self-initiated activities, confidence, and self-reliance.
8. Encourage the development of self-help skills, aceeptance of responsibility, and the ability to follow through on activities. The child should quickly be involved with and become responsible for putting away any toys and clothing, for dressing and toilet activities, and for assisting other family members in the routines of daily living.
9. Be attentive to the development of good listening and communication skills. Actively listen to your child and encourage expression of thoughts and feelings both verbally and nonverbally. The tiny toddler with limited language can still graphically relate the experience of watching daddy's plane land at the airport or the duck feeding in a pond or even the sad tale of a bird flying into a picture window—complete with appropriate facial expressions and sound effects.
10. Encourage your child's sensitivity to and empathy for the needs of others. Gifted children tend to be unusually aware of the feelings of others and often seem to share the intensity of the pain or joy the other is experiencing. Since this can be a traumatic event, it is important that the child be encouraged to cope with empathetic feelings in a constructive way.
11. Assist and encourage your child's special interests to the degree that the family is compatible in doing so, including such sacrifices as are willingly made. Do not feel, however, that the gifted child's interests and wishes should take precedence over all other family members and their needs.
12. Encourage your child to be self-reliant and resourceful. The gifted child can readily become his or her own best advocate in the community. Help the child early to become acquainted with community resources such as libraries, museums and other educational and vocational resources, transportation, and commu-

nication networks. Provide opportunities for mastering the skills which facilitate access to and use of such resources. Also, assist your child in becoming aware of human resources and encourage him or her to seek out others who can share special interests and/or who have the expertise to further the child's development.
13. Encourage the development of the child's natural bent for moral, ethical behavior and for community service. Gifted children usually display an intense interest in fair play and resent the unequal treatment of their peers or themselves. They also show an interest in learning which extends to the learning of others. Thus, they often make natural tutors and derive enjoyment from activities which offer little challenge to them as individuals but provide the opportunity for them to assist children younger or less able than themselves. They also readily understand philanthropic activities at an early age and get much satisfaction out of participation in community projects.

WORKING WITH PARENTS IN COUNSELING THE GIFTED

Parents of gifted children often express surprise when their children have been identified as gifted. While most are pleased to have their youngsters included in special activities or programs, they may not previously have thought of their children as being significantly different from other children of their acquaintance or their own remembered development. Often these reported perceptions are, in fact, realistic, since the children of their friends and associates and they themselves may also be gifted. For these parents, it may be only the "very highly" gifted child or the child who has had an inordinate amount of early training whose talents and achievements stand out as significantly different from their own experientially developed norms.

It is not uncommon for parents whose children have consistently earned high marks and praise for their academic achievement and social accomplishments never to have questioned the adequacy of their children's educational programs even when the children may have been working two to four years below their demonstrated achievement levels in school.

The frequency rate of failure to identify and/or seek differentiated programming for students highlights the importance of enabling parents to become aware of the characteristics of gifted children which result in needs which are uniquely different from those of most children and which may require different learning situations, teaching strategies, and programs if the child is to progress at a rate commensurate with his or her abilities.

In order for the parent to become a more effective counselor for a child, he or she must also be knowledgeable about the nature of the regular school programs and the adequacy of alternative options available (or potentially available) to his or her child and other gifted children.

All components of a program designed to train parents in counseling as a strategy should stress: (a) the individual differences inherent within all groups of children, including the gifted, (b) the need of every child to develop a feeling of self-worth, (c) awareness and sensitivity to the needs and feelings of others, and (d) the ability to interact with other children and adults in a productive manner. The designers of parent (and child) training programs must exert care to avoid encouraging or reinforcing the impression that gifted children, their parents, or mentors are either better or more deserving than other children—only that accommodations must be made to facilitate their natural rate of growth and development. The designers and implementors of parent training programs should also emphasize the need for parents to work cooperatively with the school and community in developing more optimal learning experiences for all children but should not in any way attempt to deter parents from seeking appropriate programming for gifted children.

Parents need to become well-acquainted with the myths and prejudices which affect the attitudes of teachers, administrators, and parents themselves toward gifted children and differentiated educational programs for them. Parents also often need help in coping with their feelings about having their child labeled and provided with special services. The following list, compiled by Willard Abraham (1982), provides a sample of such attitudes.

1. "Gifted children ripen early (intellectually) and rot early (emotionally)."
2. "They are so bright that they can manage to get through school without counseling."
3. "We should be satisfied if they perform adequately for their age and in the appropriate grade for their age."
4. "It is undemocratic to single them out in any way, creating a snobbish elite."
5. "They are eccentric, kind of peculiar, and have more than their share of health problems and difficulties in being with other people."
6. "Gifted and handicapped children are in separate groups... no overlap."

7. "We have to wait until past early childhood before we can identify them as being gifted."

In order to learn to deal with feelings related to their children and the school services (or lack of services) being provided them, opportunities should be provided for large and/or small group sessions which encourage a discussion of their feelings, frustrations, and perceived successes or failures in relating to their own children and/or the school environment. Groups may be encouraged to form and reform according to shared interests and concerns and to employ specialists to be familiar with special problem areas or needs.

Training in the use of such counseling tools as simulation, role-playing, and social drama can be helpful to parents in developing new insights and possible alternative approaches to parent/child interactions. Parents may in turn use these techniques within the family setting to assist other family members in becoming more aware of the dynamics of family interactions.

Communication skills employed by professional counselors can be especially valuable to parents in helping their children to understand themselves in relation to their present and future roles and surroundings. Parents thus may find the following approaches useful:

1. Giving the child invidual attention
2. Not rushing to conclusions and interpretations
3. Listening for feeling as well as content
4. Reflecting on content and feeling to confirm or clarify parent or child perception
5. Asking questions which encourage the child to communicate.

Using such communication skills will increase parent understanding of the perceptual world of the gifted child. With increased understanding, the parent will be able to develop a stronger rapport and facilitative relationship with the child.

The skills which parents refine in relating to their children as well as the insight and understanding parents gain through the improved relationship will increase their effectiveness in assisting their children in locating and making better use of school and community resources as well as by aiding the children to develop more effective communication and interpersonal skills.

Parent training programs should enable parents to become increasingly aware of and sensitive to those characteristics of gifted children which have the potential for becoming liabilities as well as assets and the problems which they may pose for gifted children and their families. As previously indicated, these include high physical and psychological energy and drive, a tendency to challenge authority, sensitivity to interpersonal relationships, a heightened awareness of feelings, and unevenness of development.

ESTABLISHING ROLE MODELS FOR THE GIFTED

Gifted children whose intellectual functioning exceeds that of other family members and/or other persons within the limits of their extended environments often have difficulty in finding suitable role models who demonstrate similar interests and a greater degree of expertise in the child's preferred interest area(s).

Some children, more fortunate than others, share the interests of a knowledgeable family member or acquaintance for whom they have considerable respect. Others are able to seek out and form satisfying relationships with persons previously known to them, their families, or acquaintances only by reputation.

Many gifted children must turn to autobiographies or biographies of eminent persons or find their heroes through the media of the press, radio, films, or TV documentaries while still others resort to emulating fictional heroes on the basis of the extraordinary achievements and accomplishments ascribed to them. However, the more remote or unrealistic (e.g., James Bond, Buck Rogers) the figure, the more difficult it is likely to be for the child to sustain the interest, motivation, and perseverance necessary in pursuing the ultimate goal of achieving some degree of authority or renown in his or her area of interest.

Interviews with persons of prominence concerning their developmental years and the persons or events which most influenced their career choices usually reveal at least one person of their acquaintance who had a significant impact on their career choices (Cox, 1926; Goertzels & Goertzels, 1962). Often this was a parent, family member, teacher, or other adult within the child's community who had attributes or interest which the child found particularly attractive.

While some eminent adults report that even relatively brief encounters with their real-life heroes were so strong that they continued to be remembered into adulthood, it would appear to be unwise to trust to chance.

A long look back in history (e.g., Plato, Aristotle) as well as at current (and recent past) mentor and internship programs suggests that such activities not only provide gifted children with the opportunity for hands-on experiences in their special interest areas but with role models which they had not previously been able to find. One youth who had been afforded a two-week period to work with a published author has maintained a mentor relationship by mail over a six-year span of time. Another child has maintained a personal relationship with each of two mentors over a similar period of time.

Parents, as well as teachers and counselors, can not only assist their gifted children in locating appropriate mentors, but also are often able to exchange roles serving as mentors or providing intern experiences for each other's children. Parents of gifted children are often much more eager to serve as resource people or mentors because they are more aware of their own children's needs to interact with persons with greater knowledge and expertise.

CONCLUSION

The parents of a gifted child are faced with many decisions regarding the child's education—decisions made more difficult by the overlay of issues of affective development. However, cooperative efforts between home and school in how to meet the counseling needs of the gifted child can help make such decisions easier.

REFERENCES

Abraham, Willard, list used with graduate classes, Arizona State University, 1982.
Colangelo, N., & Zaffrann, R., *New voices in counseling the gifted,* Dubuque IA: Kendall-Hunt Publishing Co., 1979.
Cox, B., *Genetic studies of genius* (Vol. 2). Stanford: Stanford University Press, 1926.
Delp, J., & Martinson, R. *The gifted and talented: A handbook for parents.* Ventura CA: Ventura County Superintendent of Schools, 1975.
Gallagher, J. J. *Teaching the Gifted Child,* New York: Allyn and Bacon, 1976.
Ginsberg, G. *Is your child gifted?* New York: Simon & Schuster, 1976.
Goertzelo, V., & Goertzels, S. M. *Cradles of eminence.* Boston: Little, Brown, 1962.
Gowan, J. C., & Bruch, C. *The academically talented student and guidance.* Boston: Houghton-Mifflin Co., 1971.
Kaufmann, F. *Your gifted child and you.* Reston VA: Council for Exceptional Children, 1976.

CHAPTER SEVEN

School Counseling Needs and Successful Strategies to Meet Them

Joyce VanTassel-Baska

Positive efforts on behalf of the affective needs of gifted students must occur in the school program if these students are to receive an appropriate education. Developing an understanding of self and others is critical to enhancing a gifted student's self-concept and developing appropriate motivational patterns. Small group and individual counseling sessions can provide gifted students with the opportunity to practice coping skills needed to deal with their exceptionality and provide meaningful behavioral patterns for relating to others. Such activities as role playing, discussion, and volunteer experiences with others—tutoring younger children, for example—are important.

The teacher of the gifted, along with parents, can assume a central role in guiding affective development. A recent study on nurturing the gifted suggests that a responsive environment that allows for intimate as well as continuing contacts with adults is one of the most important ingredients for affective growth (Freehill, 1978). Other writers perceive the affective needs of the gifted as parallel to Maslow's hierarchy of needs but more intensive than for other populations because of the greater perceptual awareness and sensitivity of the gifted. Lundy (1978) states that: "The gifted individual is both burdened and blessed with a complex set of capabilities and aptitudes that may be instrumental in providing self-worth or self-negating feedback" (p. 5).

Such needs of gifted students can be categorized into three major areas: psychosocial needs, skill development needs, and life planning needs. Each area of need is important at various stages in the developmental process and each should be an ongoing part of a counseling program for the gifted.

PSYCHOSOCIAL NEEDS

The gifted can be perceived as psychological misfits because they exist in a society that values conformity of behavior. Instead of celebrating and cherishing differences, society tends to amalgamate and assimilate them through its institutions. Perhaps schools, as microcosms of society, are most guilty of this attempt to standardize behavior. Because of the school's generic role in this process, it is difficult for the gifted to develop and maintain a sense of identity that does not force them to "shed" their mantle of giftedness. For gifted students, two behavioral approaches are common: withdrawal of gifted behaviors and acting out for others.

For example, Amy used to read voraciously in class when there was extra time until her peers made fun of her "nose-in-a-book" classroom behavior. After several such episodes, Amy stopped reading in class and began manifesting classroom behavior exactly like her peers—talking, daydreaming, and so on. Another student, Tim, knew he was bright, and his peers teased him because of it. Their attitude bothered him, but he decided to accentuate the issue by answering all questions asked in class, challenging the teacher, and making himself physically conspicuous in the room. Tim became a behavior problem in class to "deal" with his own giftedness.

Gifted students have many psychosocial needs that a counseling program might address to remedy the behavioral responses of the Amys and Tims in our world.

1. Gifted students need to develop appreciation for the similarities and differences between themselves and others. Too frequently, gifted students blame themselves for being different, and the lack of acceptance of those around them only intensifies their perceptions of feeling inadequate.
2. Gifted students need help in learning skills related to social adaptation. They need to understand the differences between cooper-

ation and competition, and when each mode may be appropriate. They need to understand the implications of preferring to work and play alone as those tendencies relate to making and keeping friends, social popularity, and social leadership. They also need to learn the art of compromise in order to adapt successfully in varying situations.
3. Gifted students need to know how to channel their sensitivity. Vulnerability to criticism can be devastating unless they learn ways of coping with their highly sensitive natures.
4. Gifted students need to receive an honest appraisal of their ideas and products. Too often, the gifted are never made aware of the strengths and weaknesses in their work, an awareness which is essential for growth.
5. Gifted students need to learn to assess the behavior of themselves and others objectively. Frequently the gifted have unreasonably high levels of expectations for themselves which can result in lack of self-esteem. They need to learn how to accept praise for excellence and to recognize acceptable levels of performance in different contexts.
6. Gifted students need to develop an understanding of the positive value of humor and the constructive ways it can be used. Sometimes gifted students develop the use of sarcasm or "smart alecky" responses as a defense against being hurt, thus inverting a positive characteristic for negative use.

STRATEGIES FOR MEETING PSYCHOSOCIAL NEEDS

Personnel working with the gifted can address these psychosocial needs in many ways. However, some successful strategies include:

1. Simulations and role playing activities that allow the gifted student to observe situations from an objective distance to gain insight into the behavior manifested.
2. Bibliotherapy that allows the gifted student to read about another student who is similar in respect to affective characteristics. Reference: *The Gifted Child in Literature,* National Council of Teachers of English, 1979.
3. Reading biographies about eminent adults who may have exhibited similar needs as children. Such books graphically portray how the eminent adult coped with psychosocial needs in childhood. Reference: Goertzels, V., & Goertzels, M. *Cradles of Eminence, 1962.*

4. Use of special units that conceptually address the need directly. For example, a unit on humor can be focused in such a way as to explore the delightful use of humor as a positive force in life.
5. Inquiry-based class and/or small group discussions using selected readings that reflect a similar problem in a character. Reference: Junior Great Books, The Great Books Foundation, 40 East Huron Street, Chicago, Illinois 60601.
6. Small group projects that focus on human behavior. Students may read and do research on giftedness and on creative individuals. Written and oral reports should follow. Reference: Kaplan, Sandra et al. *The Big Book of Independent Study*, Goodyear Publishing Company, 1976.
7. Formation of ongoing counseling groups organized specifically to provide gifted children with a context to discuss problems and issues related to their own affective development.

SKILL DEVELOPMENT NEEDS

As has been demonstrated in research (Colangelo & Zaffrann, 1977; Gowan, Demos, & Kokaska, 1972) gifted students do have areas of skill development with which they need assistance even to the point of remediation. The most critical of these include:

1. *Study skills.* The gifted, due to lack of challenge and practice in self-discipline, may become unmotivated in their approach to academic work. Consequently, when they begin programs or face a challenging academic situation for the first time, many do not have the study skills needed to cope with the challenge, even though they do have the ability needed to perform the expected tasks.
2. *Decision making skills.* The gifted have many more choices to make in life than average individuals, because of their varied abilities coupled with strong and versatile interest patterns. Consequently, they need the skills of decision making at their disposal at an early age.
3. *Test taking skills.* While gifted students may surface through an exceptional ability to take tests, some of these students need help in becoming test wise so that they can demonstrate their abilities in educational testing situations.

CAREER AND LIFE PLANNING NEEDS

An important key to successful counseling for gifted students lies in helping them develop a strong sense of their overall potential as well as an understanding of their special areas of talent. Alternatives and options should always be offered along with the rationale supporting the appropriateness of each option for the individual. Career choices should reflect life planning models that allow for appropriate development and growth at various junctures in the life cycle. Specific needs in this area include:

1. *Career education.* The gifted need to have a sense of career opportunities based on their tested strengths and weaknesses in aptitude areas. Knowing appropriate options for choice of a higher education institution also constitutes a related need in this area.
2. *Internship experiences.* The gifted need to explore career implications for themselves both through independent study and through first-hand experience so that choices reflect thorough research.
3. *Mentorship experiences.* The gifted need real-life role models who can provide a focus and direction at various stages of their lives. In many professions, for example, a mentor may be critical to individual advancement.

STRATEGIES FOR MEETING CAREER AND LIFE PLANNING NEEDS

It is in this area of counseling and guidance that school personnel can most effectively facilitate the needs of gifted students, since most programs already stress the importance of internships and mentorships, for reasons other than those cited here. Specific strategies that could be used to meet these needs include:

1. Community or government internships that allow students to spend one semester exploring a career area. Reference: Executive Internship Program (contact individual state coordinator for more information on state adaptation).
2. Buddy systems that match an older gifted child with a younger one for purposes of role model identification and career planning issues.
3. Use of parents and members of community groups and organizations as mentors for individual gifted children. At a

more organized level, resource directories of individuals and their specialty areas can be prepared. Reference: Mensa International.
4. Career education and mentor programs for the gifted organized in a local school district by school personnel.
5. Excursions to selected universities to allow gifted students to gain perspective on different campus situations.

CONCLUSION

While the affective needs of the gifted can be seen as diverse, so too are the strategies for addressing those needs. No one approach may necessarily be effective with a given student. The implementation of these strategies should be viewed in the context of a K–12 developmental effort so that appropriate intervention is provided as needs become apparent. Just as in other phases of program development, a provision for ongoing counseling efforts should be made by individual school districts and the educational personnel who have direct responsibility for the gifted.

REFERENCES

Colangelo, N., & Zaffrann, R. T. *New voices in counseling the gifted.* Dubuque IA: Kendall/Hunt, 1979.

Freehill, M. Nurturing steady growth of intellectual gifts. *Roeper Review,* 1978, *1,* 3–5.

Gowan, J. C., Demos, C. O., & Kokaska, C. J. *The guidance of exceptional children.* New York: David McKay, 1972.

Lundy, J. The psychological needs of the gifted. *Roeper Review,* 1978, *1,* 5–8.

CHAPTER EIGHT

The Writing, Reading, and Counseling Connection: A Framework for Serving the Gifted

Jane M. Bailey
Linda Neal Boyce
Joyce VanTassel-Baska

The list of emotional issues faced by gifted learners is long and diverse. Some of the most frequent conflicts include confusion about the meaning of giftedness, feeling different from others, feeling inadequate, striving for perfection, and maintaining positive relationships with peers (Silverman, 1988). At the classroom level it is the teacher, often untrained in specific counseling techniques, who is responsible for helping gifted students sort through these issues.

An exploration of the writing, reading, and counseling processes reveals some intriguing opportunities for meeting the affective needs of gifted learners within the context of the curriculum. All three processes operate in a similar nurturing environment, have similar structural stages, have built-in mechanisms for self-exploration, and work towards a goal of self-efficacy: creating independent writers, independent readers, and independent thinkers. If it were possible to harness these three processes so they could be used in an integrated way, a powerful framework for dealing with the affective needs of gifted learners would be available to classroom teachers, a framework which is both flexible and congruent with the daily curriculum.

WRITING PROCESS

Perhaps because of the nature of the written word, it is easier to conceptualize writing as a product-oriented subject than as a process. All too often, writing assignments are generated as vehicles to get to an end-product objective; the teacher's emphasis is on the outcome. For the gifted child in particular, an emphasis on product may exacerbate problems with perfectionism or unrealistically high self-expectations.

A process approach to writing shifts the concern from an end-position (product outcome) and spreads it throughout all writing phases. In other words, the *how* and *why* of writing become just as important as the outcome. A linear representation of writing phases demonstrates movement toward the creation of independence in writing (see Figure 2).

A writing process program offers some sound practical benefits to gifted learners: Students can proceed at their own pace, choose their own topics, use their own vocabulary, and be as creative as they choose. VanTassel-Baska (1988) suggests that writing programs for gifted students begin as soon as they enter school. A process approach enables even very young children to "write" using drawings as the basis of their stories (Hilliker, 1982). A writing process program can also span the entire K–12 curriculum. The goal is to create self-directed, independent writers.

Each phase of writing is part of a cognitive structure that helps students move forward on the continuum, and each part of the continuum provides potential opportunities for meeting varying affective needs of the gifted. *Prewriting* helps children think about what they will write and get ideas into working memory; they come to grips with an audience and a purpose. Gifted children are often so fluent in symbolic language that teachers assume they need little support in topic choice. Work with young writers in The College of William and Mary's Gifted Learner Program reveals their need for prewriting structure to help them focus on particular ideas.

The prewriting activity is meant to provide an easy transition into *composing:* the actual production of words. Ideas are put on paper with a minimum of frustration—without worrying about spelling and proofreading. For young gifted children, this freedom encourages early fluency with the written language. Free compos-

Figure 2. Writing phases.

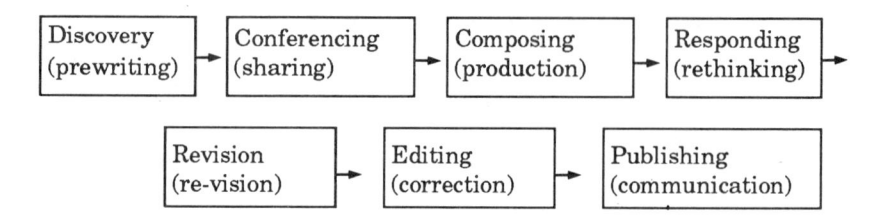

Discovery (prewriting) → Conferencing (sharing) → Composing (production) → Responding (rethinking) →

Revision (re-vision) → Editing (correction) → Publishing (communication)

ing also inhibits the striving for perfection and fear of failure. The reward structure is not based on a structurally perfect composition; rather, it is based on the process of learning how to become fluent, independent writers.

The *revising* schema is provided via a *conference* with the teacher or with other writing peers. Calkins (1983, p. 139) demonstrates the critical importance of the conference as a model for children to learn which questions to ask themselves about their writing. An effective facilitator enables children to express those parts of their writing that they really care about and uses a guided questioning technique to help writers add supportive details, delete unnecessary parts, vary sentences, or use more precise words. This emphasis on revision is helpful to gifted children who are always trying to meet some pre-set standard.

Conferencing offers several opportunities to meet affective needs in context. The one-on-one contact offers opportunities for teachers to deal with the needs of introverted students, and the peer conferencing helps gifted children learn the social skills of group interaction and develop close relationships based on the mutual need for writing feedback.

As the process unfolds, *editing* or correcting mechanical mistakes puts the manuscript into publishable form. *Publishing* enables the writer to communicate the final written piece within a public forum. Stories can be published in classroom booklets, newspapers, literary magazines, or writing displays.

Setting up a consistent structure for students to share their writing provides an audience and a forum for the critical analysis of a piece of writing. Even small children can share their stories to a group of responsive listeners. A suggested structure is to have a sharing schedule which allows each child a time to share a piece of writing with a group of other children. After reading the story, the writer can ask, "What did you like about this story?" and then

"What further information would you like about this story?" The responses of the group enable the writer to get positive feedback and suggestions for story revision. The listeners get an opportunity to analyze a piece of writing by being specific about what they liked or what information they would like added to or subtracted from a story. The teacher can stretch this critical response activity by asking respondents *why* they thought a particular part was good or needed changing.

The sharing time becomes an opportunity for peer interaction. Certainly any public forum becomes an opportunity to build a child's self-confidence. As children develop an appreciation for what others write, it helps them come to grips with the concept of giftedness as being relative to a given context, (e.g., some students are more gifted at writing than others). It also contributes to student understanding of giftedness to the extent that it is transformed into shared thought and feeling. The writing process greatly facilitates such opportunities.

A benefit of the process approach to writing is the emphasis on the importance of the child's inner self as the driving force which makes the process work. The writing process as defined by Graves (1983) uses the child's experiences, the child's language, and the child's topics. The process of prewriting, composing, revising, editing, and publishing provides a scaffold for the student to climb independently. The writing goes directly from the child's heart to the child's hand. It is the very child-centered nature of the writing process that makes it an ideal mechanism for helping gifted children come to grips with their affective needs.

READING PROCESS

As in the writing process, independence is the goal of the reading process. Most children learn to read, yet few become avid readers—readers who search for information and meaning, readers who use books to enrich their lives. To become active independent readers, most children need help in learning and constructing a reading process—a process that parallels the writing process in many respects, as shown in Figure 3.

A lifelong commitment or passion for literature seems to develop when students see a personal connection with reading and when they feel competent to interpret the text. A literature program that integrates response, reflection, and presentation shares the counseling components of bibliotherapy: the use of literature to

Figure 3. The reading process.

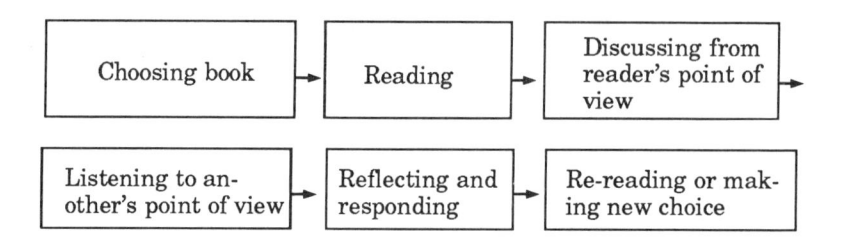

```
┌─────────────────┐   ┌─────────┐   ┌──────────────────┐
│  Choosing book  │──▶│ Reading │──▶│ Discussing from  │──▶
│                 │   │         │   │ reader's point of│
│                 │   │         │   │ view             │
└─────────────────┘   └─────────┘   └──────────────────┘

┌─────────────────┐   ┌─────────────┐   ┌──────────────────┐
│ Listening to an-│──▶│Reflecting and│──▶│ Re-reading or mak-│
│other's point of │   │responding    │   │ ing new choice   │
│view             │   │              │   │                  │
└─────────────────┘   └──────────────┘   └──────────────────┘
```

address key counseling needs. In fact, it is sometimes difficult to distinguish one from the other.

Such an experiential approach to literature is particularly suited to gifted learners because:

- It presents literature as a system rather than as fragmented skills.
- It gives the responsibility for response to the reader and respects the individual's unique interpretation and application.
- It presents a body of knowledge for gifted learners to comprehend and to use in writing and in further reading.
- It provides a framework for gifted learners to ask the ethical and moral questions that often provoke them.
- It ensures that the results of reading such as critical thinking, introspection, and personal understanding will receive regular attention rather than occasional, sporadic inclusion as a special topic in the curriculum.

Two authors who have described the reading process, Hansen (1987) and Probst (1988), enumerate its essential components. First, readers must be able to choose their own books. Just as writers choose their own content so that they care about it, own it, and can control it, so must readers select their own books in order to care about reading them. Hansen asserts that by selecting their own books, children learn to monitor their own reading strategies, and they become aware of their own reading process. If gifted children are to use literature to probe emotions and universal issues, their books must support their quest. The complexity and ambiguity gifted children face in their lives should be reflected in substantive books they choose to read. Trivial plots and characters with obvious solutions do not support thinking and reflection. Baskin and Harris (1980), Hauser and Nelson (1988), and Halsted (1988) provide extensive annotated bibliographies for selecting books to offer gifted children.

In the writing process, children are given regular times to write. They become a community of writers with the teacher as a model—the teacher writes with them and participates in each step of the process as a sympathetic guide. Likewise, in the reading process, students need regular, anticipated times to read within their community of readers.

Next, children share what they have read with their fellow readers. They have the opportunity to say what they found important, what confused them, what intrigued or angered them. Because each person has unique experiences and perspective, each person's response to a book is unique. There is no right or best response. In the words of Probst (1988), "literature is experience not information" (p. i). Hansen (1987) points out that for a response group to be effective, the group must build on one another's responses. Before offering one's own response, a group participant must "affirm and extend" (Hansen, 1987, p. 75) the initial response that was offered. Here again the reading process parallels the writing process by honoring the individual's contribution.

After affirming and extending the reader's response in a conference or group, listeners have the opportunity to offer their own reactions. Here the group members must countenance each other with conflicting viewpoints, perspectives and biases. Consensus is not the goal. Instead, listening to another's response, then using it to further one's own reflections and understanding is emphasized. At this point misreading and faulty interpretations can be addressed by the group (Probst, 1988). Listening to the responses of others and possibly even rereading for confirmation or new understanding mimics the revising stage of the writing process.

Finally, the reader chooses another book to read. Being part of a reading community provides the impetus and the ideas for another selection. Within a group of readers, students know what others have read and liked; they know why a friend chose a particular book; and they are always free to seek help and suggestions. The goal is for the students to become independent, active readers for life.

Ideally, the reading process also promotes an affective response to literature, a focusing on personal experience rather than information. Robert Coles describes the process and the results of a lifelong involvement with reading in *The Call of Stories: Teaching and the Moral Imagination* (1989). He chronicles his own involvement with books from his childhood through his careers—in medicine and psychiatry and now in the literature courses he conducts at Harvard University for prospective doctors, lawyers, and teachers. His students read the stories of people's lives in classic and current literature. As they relate their reading to their own lives and careers, they consider the moral and ethical implications. Coles describes heightened awareness, moments of understanding the meaning of life, and moral decisions reached after reading a particular book. He refers to this as the consequences of reading and responding to a story:

> Its indirections become ours. Its energy invites our own energetic leap into sadness, delight, resentment, frustration. Psychiatrists use words such as empathy, identification, introspection. . . . The whole point of stories is not 'solutions' or 'resolutions' but a broadening and even a heightening of our struggles—with new protagonists and antagonists introduced, with new sources of concern or apprehension or hope, as one's mental life accommodates itself to a series of arrivals: guests who have a way of staying, but not necessarily staying put. (p. 129)

Coles' belief that the point of stories is to broaden and heighten personal struggles echoes Ogburn-Colangelo's (1979) application of Dabrowski's theory of positive disintegration to counseling the gifted. Ogburn-Colangelo points out that it is important not for the client to resolve conflict but to be valued for having it, that emotional conflict is useful to development. Ogburn-Colangelo encourages a personal quest through counseling; Coles promotes similar personal searching by asking students to respond to stories.

BIBLIOTHERAPY

Bibliotherapy shares many of the components of a response-based literature program, and can be an accessible, natural tool for teachers and librarians as well as counselors. Gifted learners may be particularly well suited to bibliotherapy given their penchant for reading, their enthusiasm for asking questions, and their capacity for divergent thinking (Webb, Meckstroth, & Tolan, 1982). Only a few adaptations are necessary in a response-based literature program to address the personal and social needs of gifted learners.

Halsted (1988) identifies three types of bibliotherapy—institutional, clinical, and developmental. In her construct, mental health professionals use institutional and clinical bibliotherapy with clients who have emotional or behavior problems. Conversely, teachers, parents, librarians, and school counselors use developmental bibliotherapy to anticipate and meet needs before they become problems. Halsted advocates bibliotherapy as a means of helping gifted learners recognize and articulate the difficulties that surround being different and of confronting their reluctance to use their abilities.

Central to using bibliotherapy is an understanding of what it does for a reader. Halsted describes the four stages of bibliotherapy as identification, catharsis, insight, and universalization. In the first stage, a reader *identifies* with a character in the book, recognizing personal similarities and caring about the character. In explaining *catharsis*, Halsted quotes a psychological definition:

> It [catharsis] is an active release of emotions, experienced either first-hand or vicariously. Catharsis goes beyond the simple intellectual recognition of commonalities as in identification. . . . It involves empathetic emotional reactions. (p. 66)

The third stage, *insight*, occurs when the reader applies the character's situation to his or her own life. Finally, universalization is the reader's recognition that difficulties and sense of difference are not his or hers alone.

An integrated literature model addresses an additional counseling need of gifted learners: communication of feelings (Webb, Meckstroth, & Tolan, 1982). In isolation, bibliotherapy speaks to the reader's emotions and self-understanding. In the broader context of a response-based literature program, it provides a forum for practicing a range of communication skills. Students recognize, label, and honor feelings: they articulate fears; they listen and learn to reflect another's feelings; they work cooperatively; they learn to support a personal point of view; and they communicate formally with an audience through their presentation.

COUNSELING PROCESS

The process of counseling also proceeds along a continuum. Hackney and Cormier (1979) describe the importance of relating to the client (developing rapport), recognizing and attending to communication patterns, responding to the client in a cognitive context and an affective context, conceptualizing problems and setting goals, practicing intervention strategies, and restructuring behavior. A critical aspect of counseling is helping the client become independent through an acceptance of self and through learning how to make changes and adjustments (see Figure 4).

Figure 4. The counseling process.

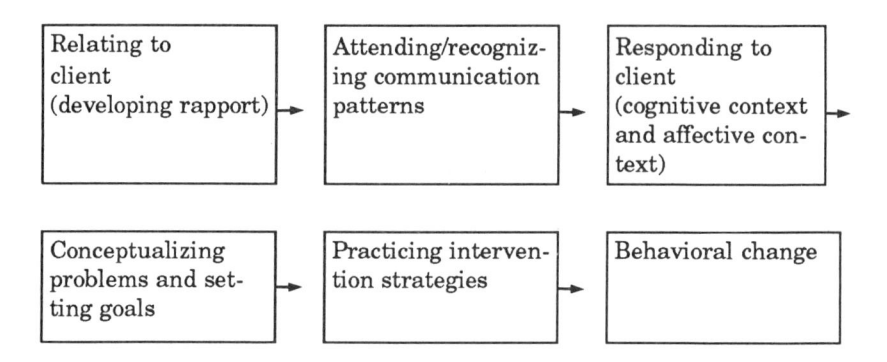

```
┌─────────────────┐   ┌─────────────────┐   ┌─────────────────┐
│ Relating to     │   │ Attending/recog-│   │ Responding to   │
│ client          │ → │ nizing communi- │ → │ client          │ →
│ (developing     │   │ cation patterns │   │ (cognitive      │
│  rapport)       │   │                 │   │  context and    │
│                 │   │                 │   │  affective      │
│                 │   │                 │   │  context)       │
└─────────────────┘   └─────────────────┘   └─────────────────┘

┌─────────────────┐   ┌─────────────────┐   ┌─────────────────┐
│ Conceptualizing │   │ Practicing      │   │ Behavioral      │
│ problems and    │ → │ intervention    │ → │ change          │
│ setting goals   │   │ strategies      │   │                 │
└─────────────────┘   └─────────────────┘   └─────────────────┘
```

For the classroom teacher, an awareness of this process is a first step in being able to use it for meeting the affective needs of gifted students through writing and literature. The importance of developing rapport with the gifted child is an important beginning stage. Such students respond well to humorous interchange, authentic dialogue, and open discussion. Silverman (1988) lists several approaches to establishing rapport with gifted children, all important avenues to explore:

- Invite person to share feelings.
- Listen.
- Ask for more information—do not assume you understand.
- Respect the problems—do not try to resolve them.
- Withhold judgments.
- Do not agree with the person continuously.
- Be authentic in your responses.
- Empathize—try to enter the student's inner world.
- Encourage the full expression of emotions.
- Support and validate the person's feelings.
- Do not take sides on the issues.
- Share common experiences—no one likes to feel alone.

Attention to a gifted child's communication pattern can yield understanding of how the child thinks and feels about self as well as about the world. The teacher must be sensitive to both verbal and nonverbal cues and use them to help a child deal with special problems. Just because a child demonstrates a high cognitive ability and displays it confidently in a given context does not mean that affective problems are not present. Many such children betray how they feel in nonverbal ways or through more introspective processes like writing or drawing. The counseling process is a way to uncover the contextual complexity of the gifted and provide support.

At the level of responding to cognitive and affective cues, the teacher employs appropriate curriculum interventions as the primary tool. This chapter strongly suggests the use of both the writing process and the reading process in various forms as key ways to respond to both cognitive and affective needs of the gifted child, a purpose analogous to a counselor employing specific counseling strategies to respond to client content.

Problem finding and goal setting are processes central to effective counseling. Helping a client define his or her own problem, take responsibility for it, and move beyond it through taking positive steps to address it are important aspects of growth through counseling. In a similar way, a teacher, through the writing-reading connection, can help a student "work through" an issue or problem in the context of a discussion or conference, as well as introduce a means of expression that can help students articulate affective concerns.

The importance of "practicing behavior" in the counseling process is another critical stage. It is not sufficient for a client only to talk about problems; he or she must be able to act on them in some way over time. Again, the teacher of the gifted is in a position to provide appropriate expressive channels to use for problem solving and practicing "safe" behaviors through constructing hypothetical situations open to the discussion of peers.

The goal of the counseling process, like that of the writing-reading process, is positive change in the direction of self-efficacy. Clients emerge from counseling more confident of their abilities to handle problems and more sure of who they are. The use of writing and reading as key educational processes in the development of gifted children have similar goals—greater independence in thought and feeling.

WRITING, READING, AND COUNSELING CONNECTIONS

By examining the similarities among the writing, reading, and counseling processes, interconnected possibilities emerge for helping gifted students deal with social-emotional concerns. All three processes are student centered: the writing ideas and content are generated from within the writer; the reading lists are chosen and discussed by the reader; the experiences and issues to be grappled with are expressed by the student.

Throughout all three processes, the teacher or counselor is really a facilitator (Rogers, 1983). The teacher asks the writer, "What do *you* want to write about?"; the reader or counselee, "What do *you* want to talk about?" Questions are open-ended to maximize response (see Table 3). All three processes draw on the inner feelings of the child by providing appropriate avenues for emotional expression. Moreover, the outcome of all three processes is similar; self-efficacy for the learner is the desired outcome (see Figure 5).

Table 3. Parallel process questions.

	Writing	*Reading*	*Counseling*
Opening	What are you writing about today?	What do you want to read about today?	What would you like to talk about today?
Focus	What do you especially like about your story?	What strikes you as important in this book?	Why is that important to you?
Identification	What do you think makes that part of your story so good?	Which character is the most interesting? Why? How do you feel like or unlike that person?	What do you identify with in the following situation?
Generalization	What ideas do you most want to convey to your readers/audience?	If you had to describe your book in three words, what would they be and why?	What associations come to mind in regard to the situation you just described?
Hypothesis	What if you changed the ending of your story? How would that affect it?	If you were faced with the character's situation in the book, what would you do?	If you were in a given situation, what would you do?

Figure 5. Overlapping processes and outcomes for writing, reading, and counseling.

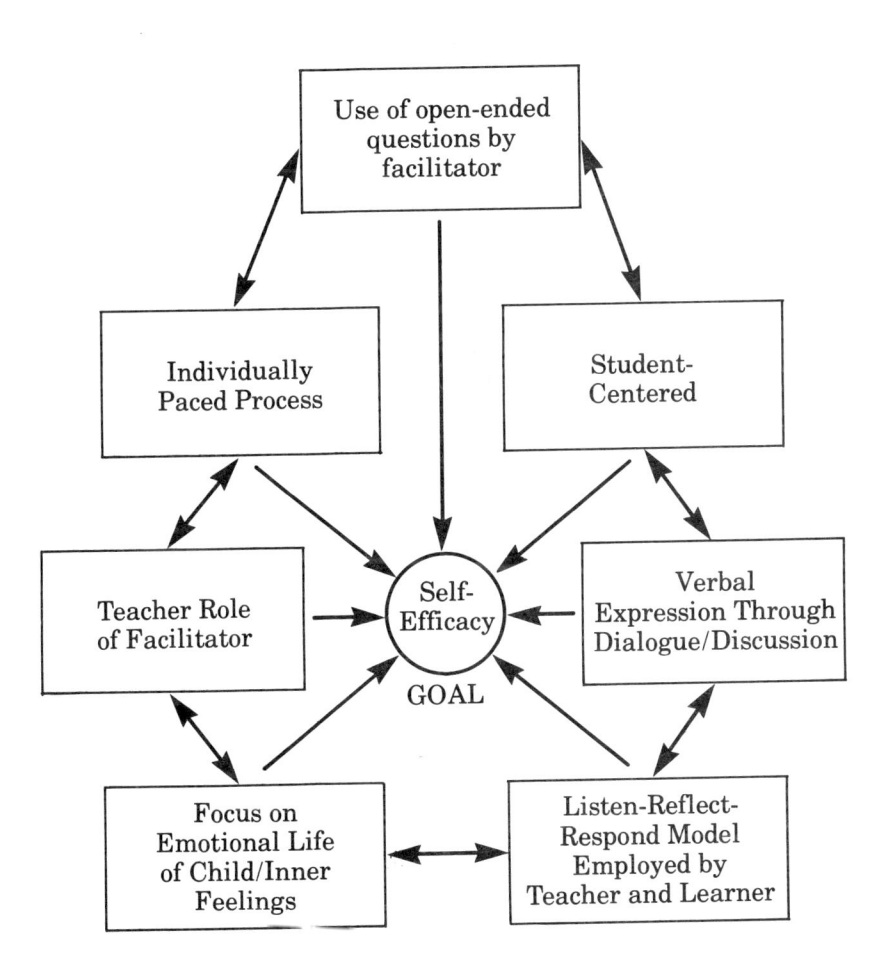

```
            ┌─────────────────┐
            │ Use of open-ended│
            │   questions by  │
            │    facilitator  │
            └─────────────────┘
       ↙            ↓            ↘
┌──────────────┐              ┌──────────────┐
│ Individually │              │   Student-   │
│ Paced Process│              │   Centered   │
└──────────────┘              └──────────────┘
     ↕              ( Self-         ↕
┌──────────────┐   Efficacy )  ┌──────────────────┐
│ Teacher Role │  ← GOAL →    │ Verbal           │
│of Facilitator│              │ Expression Through│
└──────────────┘              │ Dialogue/Discussion│
     ↕                         └──────────────────┘
┌──────────────┐              ┌──────────────────┐
│  Focus on    │              │ Listen-Reflect-  │
│Emotional Life│  ←────────→  │  Respond Model   │
│of Child/Inner│              │   Employed by    │
│   Feelings   │              │Teacher and Learner│
└──────────────┘              └──────────────────┘
```

The writing conferences help children express, expand, and clarify their thoughts. They learn to ask their own questions about writing (Calkins, 1983). The reading conferences help children clarify thoughts about their reading as they describe what they know about what they have read (Hansen, 1987, p. 38). They learn to ask themselves questions about what they have read. Counseling provides an oral forum for inner thought, expression, and clarification (Shertzer & Stone, 1980).

Another interesting parallel among the three processes is that all three provide the learner with a listening audience. The astute listener, that is, teacher or facilitator, will be able to use these processes in an interactive way. Because the writing process enables a child to write from the heart, and the reading process enables a child to verbalize feelings, several glimpses are presented to the teacher of the inner workings of a child's mind. By peering in these windows of expression, the classroom teacher is given an opportunity to monitor the emotional issues with which a gifted child may be grappling.

Case Study

Brock was a bright, self-assured 6-year-old—outgoing, popular, and a natural leader. He was a first-grader in a writing-process class when he wrote:

> I was climbing a big tree.
> I was climbing a bigger one.
> I fell and killed myself.
> Here's me buried.
> Here's me buried again.
> Here's my dust.
> Here's all my dust.

Taken at face value, Brock has written a simple narrative. But looking at the story as a window into Brock, the teacher is faced with a clue to some inner turmoil. When the teacher is told that Brock's mother has died just prior to the beginning of the school year, the fog on the window clears. Indeed Brock has revealed some of his innermost conflicts. Not long after the tree story, Brock wrote:

> Here's me sleeping.
> Here's me drowning.
> Here's my dad looking for me.
> The Coast Guard is looking for me.
> My dad felt sad.

The teacher has another window into a hurting child. When the child is as healthy and happy-looking as Brock was on the outside, windows to the inside child may be helpful. The outward self-assured appearance of many gifted children may belie the inward reality of emotional need. In this case, the teacher sought the school counselor since more affective support seemed warranted.

But more than just providing a glimpse into the child, the processes of writing and reading offer the teacher ways to meet varying affective needs on multiple levels. Table 4 aligns key affective issues of the gifted with responsive activities in writing and reading.

Table 4. Relationship of affective needs of gifted children to key interventions in writing and literature.

Selected Affective Needs of Gifted Children	Responsive Strategies of the Writing Process	Selected Books to Read and Discuss
Dealing with perfectionism fear of failure	• focusing on process that stresses and rewards rewriting and editing • assigning open-ended writing (where format and content is not set—no standard for correct response)	*Feelings* (Aliki) *Tales for the Perfect Child* (Heide) *Be a Perfect Person in Just Three Days* (Manes)

Understanding giftedness
   feelings of being different
   coping skills
   need for risk taking
	• clarifying and articulating experiences
	• publishing
	• striving for excellence—display of peer group talent
	• trying something new and different with writing techniques, ideas, format
		Miss Rumphius (Cooney)
		Wrinkle in Time (L'Engle)
		Dorp Dead (Cunningham)

Developing relationships and social skills	• conferencing and workshopping techniques with peers • sharing your writing in a public forum/group setting • developing collaborative product (journal, newspaper, collections of written stories)	*Island of the Skog* (Kellogg) *A Girl Called Al* (Greene) *The Planet of Junior Brown* (Hamilton)

(Continued)

Table 4. Relationship of affective needs of gifted children to key interventions in writing and literature.
(Continued)

Selected Affective Needs of Gifted Children	Responsive Strategies of the Writing Process	Selected Books to Read and Discuss
Introversion communication	• allowing for individual expression of ideas in a protected environment • promoting one-to-one sharing of ideas with teacher • promoting reflection and introspection as part of the writing process • providing opportunity to articulate thoughts, get feedback and test ideas, feelings against another's reality	*The 329th Friend* (Sharmat) *The Bat-Poet* (Jarrell) *Solitary Blue* (Voight)
Too high expectations of self and others	• emphasis on improvement and development as an ongoing process rather than the value of a single product	*Pezzettino* (Lionni) *And This is Laura* (Conford) *Dreams and Drummers* (Smith)
Getting in touch with inner self	• exploring experiences, feelings	*The Big Orange Splot* (Pinkwater) *A Bridge to Terabithia* (Paterson) *Very Far Away From Anywhere Else* (LeGuin)
Sensitivity toward others Tolerance	• listening to another point of view • sharing time	*Sam, Bangs, & Moonshine* (Ness) *Summer of the Swans* (Byars) *A Begonia for Miss Applebaum* (Zindel)

In the case of Brock, writing did give the teacher a glimpse of an inner reality that was inconsistent with external appearance. But the writing process may also have provided a chance for Brock to grapple with his distress in another medium; the writing itself may have been cathartic and may have helped him clarify his experiences with his mother's death. Guided reading experiences might also have provided a similar healthy release.

CONCLUSION

Brock's story offers an example of how the three processes of writing, reading, and counseling can work together to meet affective needs. By capturing opportunities to meet varying affective needs as they arise and in the context of the curriculum, the teacher may be able to facilitate a child's journey to self-understanding and self-efficacy.

REFERENCES

Baskin, B. H., & Harris, K. H. (1980). *Books for the gifted child*. New York: R. R. Bowker.

Calkins, L. M. (1983). *Lessons from a child*. Portsmouth, NH: Heinemann Educational Books.

Coles, R. (1989). *The call of stories: Teaching and the moral imagination*. Boston: Houghton Mifflin.

Graves, D. H. (1983). *Writing: Teachers and children at work*. Exeter, NH: Heinemann Educational Books.

Hackney, H., & Cormier, L. (1979). *Counseling strategies and objectives* (2nd ed.) Englewood Cliffs, NJ: Prentice-Hall.

Halsted, J. W. (1988). *Guiding gifted readers from preschool through high school: A handbook for parents, teachers, counselors and librarians*. Columbus, OH: Ohio Psychology.

Hansen, J. (1987). *When writers read*. Portsmouth, NH: Heinemann Educational Books.

Hansen, J., Newkirk, T., & Graves, D. H., (Eds.). (1985). *Breaking ground: Teachers relate reading and writing in the elementary school*. Portsmouth, NH: Heinemann Educational Books.

Hauser, P., & Nelson, G. A. (1988). *Books for the gifted child* (Vol. 2). New York: R. R. Bowker.

Hilliker, J. (1982). Labelling to beginning narrative. In T. Newkirk & N. Atwell (Eds.), *Understanding writing* (pp. 13–22). Chelmsford, MA: The Northeast Regional Exchange, Inc.

Ogburn-Colangelo, M. K. (1979). Giftedness as multilevel potential: A clinical example. In N. Colangelo & R. T. Zaffrann (Eds.), *New directions in counseling the gifted* (pp. 165–187). Dubuque, IA: Kendall/Hunt.

Probst, R. E. (1988). *Response and analysis: Teaching literature in junior and senior high school.* Portsmouth, NH: Heinemann Educational Books.

Rogers, C. R. (1983). *Freedom to learn for the 80's.* Columbus, OH: Charles E. Merrill.

Shertzer, B., & Stone, S. (1980). *Fundamentals of counseling* (3rd ed.). Boston: Houghton Mifflin.

Silverman, L. K. (1988). Affective curriculum for the gifted. In J. VanTassel-Baska, J. Feldhusen, K. Seeley, G. Wheatley, L. Silverman, & W. Foster (Eds.), *Comprehensive curriculum for gifted learners* (pp. 335–355). Boston: Allyn & Bacon.

Smith, J. A. (1967). *Creative teaching of the language arts.* Boston: Allyn & Bacon.

Stauffer, R. G. (1970). *The language-experience approach to the teaching of reading.* New York: Harper & Row.

VanTassel-Baska, J. (1988). Verbal arts for the gifted. In J. VanTassel-Baska, J. Feldhusen, K. Seeley, G. Wheatley, L. Silverman, & W. Foster (Eds.), *Comprehensive curriculum for gifted learners* (pp. 153–189). Boston: Allyn & Bacon.

Webb, J. T., Meckstroth, E. A., & Tolan, S. S. (1982). *Guiding the gifted child: A practical source for parents and teachers.* Columbus, OH: Ohio Psychology.

REFERENCES: CHILDREN'S BOOKS

Aliki. (1984). *Feelings.* New York: Greenwillow.

Byars, B. (1970). *Summer of the swans.* New York: Viking.

Conford, L. (1977). *And this is Laura.* Boston: Little, Brown.

Cooney, B. (1982). *Miss Rumphius.* New York: Viking.

Cunningham, J. (1965). *Dorp dead.* New York: Pantheon.

Greene, C. C. (1969). *A girl called Al.* New York: Viking.

Hamilton, V. (1971). *The planet of Junior Brown.* New York: Macmillan.

Heide, F. (1985). *Tales for the perfect child.* New York: Lothrop, Lee and Shepard.

Jarrell, R. (1963). *The bat-poet.* New York: Macmillan.

Kellogg, S. (1973). *Island of the Skog.* New York: Dial.

L'Engle, M. (1962). *A wrinkle in time.* New York: Farrar, Straus and Giroux.

LeGuin, U. K. (1976). *Very far away from anywhere else.* New York: Atheneum.

Lionni, L. (1975). *Pezzettino.* New York: Pantheon.

Manes, S. (1982). *Be a perfect person in just three days!* Boston: Houghton Mifflin.

Ness, E. (1966). *Sam, Bangs & Moonshine*. New York: H. Holt and Company.
Paterson, K. (1977). *A bridge to Terabithia*. New York: Crowell.
Pinkwater, D. M. (1977). *The big orange splot*. New York: Hastings.
Sharmat, M. W. (1979). *The 329th friend*. New York: Macmillan.
Smith, D. (1978). *Dreams and drummers*. New York: Crowell.
Voight, C. (1983). *Solitary blue*. New York: Atheneum.
Zindel, P. (1989). *A begonia for Miss Applebaum*. New York: Harper & Row.

CHAPTER NINE

Educational Therapy for the Gifted: The Chicago Approach

Leland K. Baska

While all mental health professionals who work for schools would like to provide unconditional assistance in meeting their client's needs, the job description for such individuals in public schools often interferes with a strict adherence to this practice. Case loads are heavy, and the roles to be performed many. What kind of counseling, then, can be delivered in a public school context?

It would seem that the essence of what schools are about, educational therapy, should be the focus of the service. Emphasis on placement, support, encouragement, and development of the breadth and depth of the child's potential is that which the school can best deliver while using the counselor as advocate and confidante for the child. Knowing how and when to refer the child's problems to outside resources and finding the right educational milieu in which the child's potential will flourish are no small accomplishments in that setting. The gifted child, in particular, by virtue of high educational potential, is best suited to this type of educational therapy and perhaps best able to develop cognitive strategies for making informed choices that will result in better adjustment.

THE CHICAGO MODEL OF EDUCATIONAL THERAPY

The Chicago Public Schools have developed and expanded a multidimensional approach for meeting the needs of its gifted population.

Central to its operation is a strong counseling component, carried out by full-time trained personnel in the areas of school psychology and social work who provide one-to-one services to gifted students and their families upon request.

In addition to the central counseling thrust, over 400 programs ranging from kindergarten to college are offered to those children identified as gifted from the 429,000 students in the system. Four full-time coordinators, along with eight pupil personnel staff members, assist local schools in developing such gifted programs through inservice training and information sharing relative to identification, administrative arrangements, curriculum, and evaluation. The gifted staff is clustered by specialty in four regional offices throughout the city so that a full range of services can be provided in a given geographical area, from program development to individual testing to family counseling.

Social workers and psychologists in these regional offices receive and follow up on referrals from other social workers and psychologists in the system as well as parents, administrators, and teachers in local schools. Types of service provided by this team include:

1. Individual and group testing with follow-up assessment of appropriate program placement.
2. Consultation on, and monitoring of, identification procedures for all gifted programs in the system.
3. Development of Individual Educational Programs (IEP's) for selected students.
4. Provision for educational program intervention.
5. Individual or group counseling for gifted children whose emotional problems are interfering with their social or academic adjustment.
6. Consultation with parents of gifted children.
7. Consultation with school administrators and teachers on affective development issues as they may relate to the education of gifted students.
8. Provision of liaison services to community agencies.

CHICAGO GIFTED PROGRAM PROTOTYPES

The educational options provided by the Chicago gifted program include many prototypes in respect to grouping and program focus. Full-day gifted magnet schools in which children are selected from several districts for homogeneous grouping are one such prototype.

The focus of these programs is breadth and depth in core content areas while offering special language, science, art, and logic courses for further enrichment. Admission is based on achievement scores at the 90th percentile and intelligence test data either from individual or group testing.

All-city programs in local museums constitute a learning laboratory of unlimited resources for high school students with access to libraries, collections, documents, workshops, and the expertise of the professional staff. These also include the study of the museum itself as an institution and its goals as a community facility. Students meet one afternoon a week and receive academic credit for their participation. Selection is made on the basis of principal and teacher recommendations, application essay, and standardized test data. Museology programs are conducted at such Chicago landmarks as the Art Institute, Field Museum, Museum of Science and Industry, and the Chicago Historical Society.

Other all-city programs include band and orchestra, an all-city chorus, and a radio broadcasting program, "Spotlight on the Gifted," which features selected programs and topics about the Chicago Gifted Program.

Local elementary school programs offer a number of program options in which inservice, curriculum, and materials are closely defined for the subject. These include: Junior Great Books; Unified Mathematics; Man: A Course of Study; Introductory Physical Science; Philosophy for Children; and the Story Workshop. By combining grades 1–2, 3–4, 5–6, and 7–8, comprehensive gifted centers have been created in some of the larger schools that allow for all-day homogeneous grouping of gifted students within a school. Advanced placement courses and several humanities programs are included as part of the high school curriculum, and recently Chicago has added the International Baccalaureate program to its offerings at selected sites.

Most individual local school programs grew out of local school needs and interests, with a teacher willing to develop a proposal and an administrator who would help implement a gifted program. Writing, art, and various other topics are included among these.

A counseling component is included as a standard part of each school's program for implementation by the teacher. Thus, summer inservice programs for teachers include considerable discussion of general characteristics of gifted students and case examples of counseling strategies that have proven successful. Social workers and psychologists also serve children in these programs as well as others who are referred. The development of counseling models that can be implemented by teachers has been effective in bringing service to more students.

University based programs are offered to junior-high-age students who have met a minimum score criterion on the Scholastic Aptitude Test (SAT), given in the spring to all students in the system who are at the 95th percentile or higher on the Iowa Test of Basic Skills (ITBS), mathematics or verbal sections. These programs are offered on school time once a week at three universities in the city: Chicago State University, Loyola University, and the University of Illinois, Circle Campus. The content offered includes Latin, creative writing, and algebra.

An overview of the programs and services model for the Chicago Gifted Program can be seen in Figure 6.

Figure 6. Chicago program prototypes.

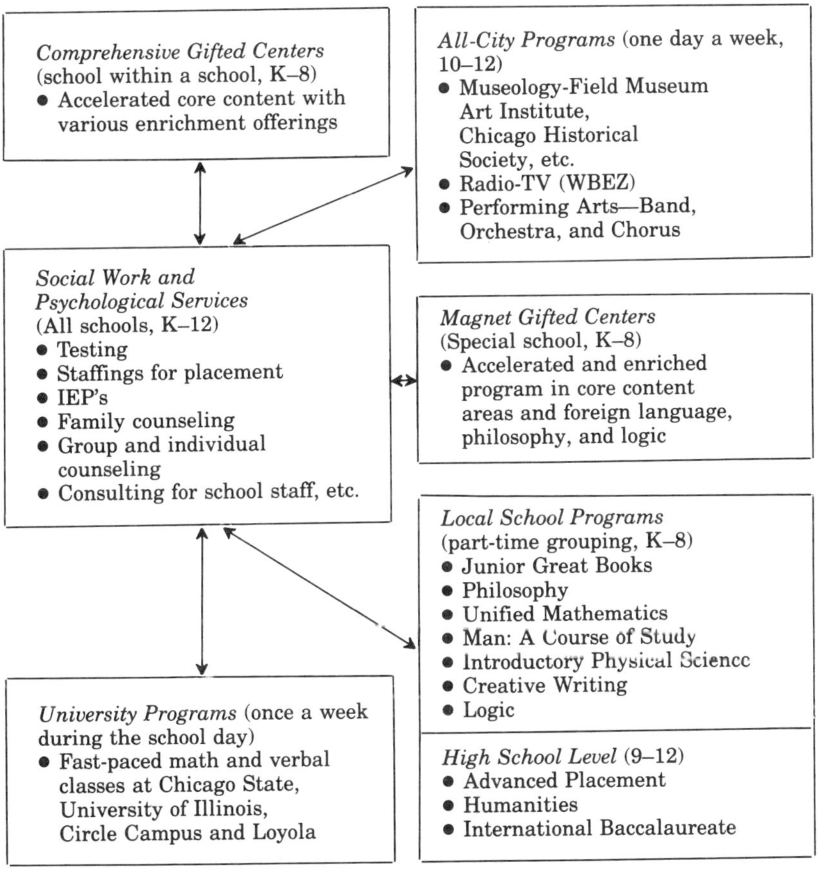

Comprehensive Gifted Centers
(school within a school, K–8)
- Accelerated core content with various enrichment offerings

All-City Programs (one day a week, 10–12)
- Museology-Field Museum Art Institute, Chicago Historical Society, etc.
- Radio-TV (WBEZ)
- Performing Arts—Band, Orchestra, and Chorus

Social Work and Psychological Services
(All schools, K–12)
- Testing
- Staffings for placement
- IEP's
- Family counseling
- Group and individual counseling
- Consulting for school staff, etc.

Magnet Gifted Centers
(Special school, K–8)
- Accelerated and enriched program in core content areas and foreign language, philosophy, and logic

Local School Programs
(part-time grouping, K–8)
- Junior Great Books
- Philosophy
- Unified Mathematics
- Man: A Course of Study
- Introductory Physical Science
- Creative Writing
- Logic

University Programs (once a week during the school day)
- Fast-paced math and verbal classes at Chicago State, University of Illinois, Circle Campus and Loyola

High School Level (9–12)
- Advanced Placement
- Humanities
- International Baccalaureate

In local schools without special programs much of the educational therapy for the gifted may take the form of recreating the best aspects of the one-room schoolhouse. Flexible programming of children at their functional levels has long been a successful strategy for schools to attempt to meet the needs of the gifted. For the low incidence, highly gifted child this may take the form of early enrollment in high school, college courses, or other adaptations.

INDIVIDUAL APPROACHES

Beyond educational therapy offered by placement in one of the gifted programs described, additional needs are frequently addressed through a specific counseling program. This includes individual counseling around particular problems and group counseling in gifted magnet programs. Educational tutoring has also been an effective tool.

The following two individual cases of gifted children illustrate the approaches taken by the Chicago Gifted Program personnel to meet the needs of individual gifted students who might otherwise be lost in a large system.

Child A is bright but has few special opportunities in his school or community, a rather lackluster academic performance, and few friends among his peers. He was 12 years old and about to enter 8th grade in an inner city school that had a gifted art program but no academic one. He was from a single parent family with a severely retarded aunt also in the mother's care. An older sister had entered a state university the year prior and the resources of the family were limited, though the mother was active in school organizations and showed determination and persistence when it came to the education of her children.

This young man showed cognitive strengths on the Stanford-Binet while achievement scores in reading and spelling were only at grade level. Computation skills for math were at 7th grade level. Against a backdrop of 138 IQ, it seemed that some form of tutoring or special program would be necessary to bring skill development into line with his potential. The usual strategy would be to find a teacher or advocate for the child in the school who is familiar with the dynamics and resources within the faculty. In this case, no such advocate was found so the psychologist for gifted programs assumed the task.

Tutoring in math was scheduled on a one hour a week basis using the programmed instructional material from Educulture, Inc. Topics of polynomial arithmetic and factoring in algebra are handled in such a way that the child can develop skill by moving through the audio tape and text at his own pace with minimal knowledge of math demanded of the counselor or person who assists him.

The plan was to develop a background of skills for high school algebra while meeting with and encouraging his teachers to enrich his course of study. The mother was encouraged to apply for scholarships for the boy through A Better Chance (ABC) Foundation. Child A is now on scholarship at an Eastern prep school and a member of the honor society there.

Child B *exemplifies the low incidence, highly gifted child and the extreme measures that must be considered for appropriate programming. He was referred at age 11 as the result of an individual examination by a local school psychologist. The IQ estimate was 165 + on the Stanford-Binet. All achievements were at the 12th grade level on the Peabody Individual Achievement Test (PIAT), and the child had consistently been at the 99th percentile on yearly standardized tests.*

Child B came from a family that valued education and provided many early experiences with formal learning within the home setting. Both parents and an older sibling offered various forms of academic stimulation. The school principal was sensitive to the boy's high ability, but also more concerned with "evening out" his ability; thus, child B took social science offerings through the early enrollment program at the local high school even though his tested strength was math. He was encouraged to take additional advanced courses at that high school and a university which he did at an "A" proficiency level.

At the completion of 8th grade, he took the pre-calculus sequence at an Eastern university so that he could enroll in Advanced Placement Calculus as a freshman. Having completed 12 hours of high school work including AP English and Chemistry, he was unable to enter the university of his choice since the minimum age admission is 15 years, but he was accepted at another university this summer for further work. He will petition for his high school diploma after a successful semester in college.

Counseling consisted of making the parents aware of a variety of options and acting as a buffer with administrators to ensure his appropriate progression through the system. Individual opportunities emerged for the child out of a persistent nature and the strong support of the family unit.

CONCLUSION

The Chicago Public Schools provide a counseling component in their gifted program that acts as a centerpeice to program development at many levels. While providing services to schools on a variety of issues, full-time psychologists and social workers also provide individual assistance to identified gifted children needing special provisions. Such specialized services also seek to encourage teachers to work on counseling needs of the gifted in individual building programs.

CHAPTER TEN

A Model for Counseling the Gifted at the High School Level

Ron Seegers

The counseling component surfaces as an integral element of programming during the high school years. While acceleration and enrichment continue to be advantageous program approaches for high school students identified as gifted, students in this age group begin to inquire about how to succeed academically, how best to prepare for college, and what careers can best suit the individual's needs and interests. The counseling program at Homewood-Flossmoor High School includes guidance in the areas of course selection, career research, and a formalized college search. Students identified as gifted work closely with a teacher-counselor to develop a personalized program that has meaning and benefit to each student.

THE SCHOOL DISTRICT

The community served by Homewood-Flossmoor High School is an educationally supportive community, represented by a widely diverse population. Generally, the community is thought of as a "white collar" suburban community, located on a major commuter line about 25 miles south of the Chicago Loop. Sociologically termed a bedroom community, its 37 thousand residents rely heavily on proximity to Chicago for both economic strength and social activity. The excellent quality of education in the public schools was one of the major factors in its rapid population growth during the period of the late 1960's and residents continually list the quality of the schools in the community as one of the most important reasons for their location in the community. Economically, the community is comfortable, reporting a mean family income of $32,000 in 1981. Many of the parents whose children attend the high school are college educated. As would be anticipated in a community of this type, the professions are well represented among the residents. Likewise, the goals of the children frequently include college and their own preparation for highly regarded professions.

The high school, founded in 1959, underwent rapid growth in the late 1960's, a leveling of population in the early to mid-1970's, and a population decline beginning in the late 1970's. The peak of 3,950 students attained in 1974 declined to a present enrollment of 2,717 students. Further decline at a decreased rate is anticipated throughout the remainder of the 1980's.

The school's reputation for excellence in education is widespread. In the *Chicago Tribune*'s selection of the 10 best suburban high schools some two years ago, Homewood-Flossmoor High School was listed. More recently, the *Chicago Sun-Times* selected the school as one of six suburban schools "that works." Several major colleges and universities, such as Tulane University and the University of Chicago, have identified the high school as one which prepares its students well for work at the university level. Among the local high schools in the south suburban area, it is recognized as a leader in academic preparation and is recognized for the rigorous program it provides its students.

THE NATURE OF THE PROGRAM

The counseling program for gifted students began at the high school in 1976. Since that time, the program has been revised and expanded. Currently its goals suggest the direction of the program. Those five goals are:

1. Students will enroll in academic programs which are commensurate with their intellectual abilities.
2. Students will enroll in classroom programs which further their identified interests.
3. Students will explore career possibilities as they relate to their abilities and interests.
4. Students will examine colleges and universities which can satisfy their academic needs and interests.

5. Students will be involved in independent learning experiences which extend beyond the usual classroom experience.

An examination of these goals suggests that implementation can best be effected by an in-depth program directed at the specific needs of gifted students. The teacher-counselor in the program meets with students frequently in a counseling role. Meetings are scheduled for both groups of students and individual students to facilitate the component of counseling for gifted students. Group meetings by year in school or class occur approximately three times per year. Individual appointments, which may occur infrequently during the first year of high school, increase in frequency as the student approaches the conclusion of the junior year. These individual conferences become most frequent during the first half of the senior year when the process of college application is in full force. Appointments with parents of gifted students are held upon request at times considered to be mutually agreeable.

Counseling in the area of academic preparation becomes the dominant focus of attention during the students' first two years of high school. The teacher-counselor spends considerable time with freshmen and sophomore students identified as gifted, planning four-year programs of study which are termed college preparatory and rigorous. With more than 75% of students at the high school anticipating further educational preparation following graduation from high school, the general curriculum can be termed college preparatory. For their four years of high school, gifted students are guided to enroll in programs which best prepare them for admission to highly competitive schools across the nation. Such considerations as in-depth study of academic areas preclude enrollment in elective courses.

Grade weighting and course leveling found throughout the curriculum have provided many options for gifted students. Likewise, gifted students have found that these processes have improved their standing since they themselves stress the need for accelerated study. All academic courses offered in the school are offered at the honors level and most other areas of study and performance provide a selection of honors programs. Additionally, students may prepare for one of ten advanced placement courses offered in the curriculum. It is expected that gifted students will enroll in at least two advanced placement courses during their studies at the high school.

Unique among the options for gifted students is the opportunity for students in the elementary schools to enroll in select high school courses while still in attendance at the junior high school. Students whose performance is deemed unusually accelerated are provided with the opportunity to enroll in one or two high school courses in areas such as mathematics and foreign language. A cooperative agreement with the elementary schools provides spaces in high school classes for able junior high school students. Transportation between schools is provided cooperatively by the elementary and high school districts. Such acceleration tends to produce students who complete programs at the high school prior to graduation. These students are then provided the opportunity to enroll in limited studies at the college level while completing their high school program. The local community college and the University of Chicago have provided classes in mathematics and foreign language for students who have completed Advanced Placement Calculus and/or Advanced Placement Spanish before the completion of their high school program. Private tutorial programs for such accelerated students are currently under consideration as an additional tool for the student who needs particular assistance.

For the student whose program cannot be optimally satisfied by the classes provided in the school curriculum or through acceleration at the college level, the district has developed a unique program of individualized study termed "the Senior Gifted Option." Students in their senior year may design a program to meet their own particular needs. During their second semester of study in the senior year, these students may participate in a program of their own design which includes such components as higher level study, pre-professional acquisition, or almost any pursuit in which they demonstrate interest. The senior designs a program with the assistance of the teacher-counselor during the first semester with implementation occurring during the second semester.

The teacher-counselor has also placed considerable emphasis on testing and preparation for testing. Far too often students are unfamiliar with the varieties of college placement tests which will be required of them prior to acceptance to college. This element of the counseling component seeks to prepare students to perform optimally on all examinations of a national scope. The teacher-counselor has developed two group sessions during the students' second year on the interpretation of test data. The way colleges look upon test scores is also clarified. Films, filmstrips, and outlines provided by Educational Testing Service and similar organizations are shown to students during after-school sessions which attempt to demonstrate the value of national tests and the manner in which students can best prepare for them. Most significantly, the students are informed of the value of preparing for such exams.

Early in the sophomore year, students are encouraged to participate in the Preliminary Scholastic Aptitude Test (PSAT) administered during October. The experience gained in testing is valuable in and of itself; however, students have the opportunity to gain a better understanding of their capabilities at the same time. Late in December, each participating student receives a summary of test scores and an evaluation of each answer given. On the basis of this performance, students are encouraged to attend one or more in a series of twelve workshops, each designed to help the student prepare for the PSAT/NMSQT (National Merit Scholarship Qualifying Test) to be taken during the following year. The workshop outline is provided to the students prior to its beginning and, in consultation with the teacher-counselor, those sessions deemed most valuable to the student's improvement are identified. Scheduled in the evenings during late winter and early spring, these sessions focus on specific sections of the test. The final two sessions instruct students in the "art" of test-taking.

Students are also instructed in the purposes and uses of the Scholastic Aptitude Test (SAT) and American College Testing Program Examination (ACT) examinations. Suggestions are made for the optimum time for attempting the exams and what alternatives are available should the student not perform well on the exam. Students seem most confused by the SAT Achievement Tests which are required for admission at highly selective schools. The teacher-counselor spends group and individual meeting time discussing the value of these exams, what exams are available to take, which exams would be appropriate for the student to attempt, and when the optimum time is to attempt such exams.

College search activities dominate much of the time the teacher-counselor spends with students during their junior and senior years. Cited as the second most important decision a student will make in his or her lifetime, the choice of college frequently is not given careful thought or planning by gifted students. They may tend to underestimate their potential for success at college. They believe that students in other schools are better equipped to compete at the most selective schools, not recognizing their own innate ability to succeed. The teacher-counselor therefore attempts through various means to help these students realize their full potential to succeed when placed with others of similar ability and to interest students in examining highly selective schools. Some specific approaches include:

1. Meeting with second year students to discuss campus visits during a family-planned summer vacation. Suggestions are given for the kinds of questions to be asked, things to look for in curricular opportunities and living conditions, etc.
2. Encouraging attendance at the annually scheduled college night

on the high school campus each fall. Some 150 colleges and universities from throughout the country attend, providing information and literature about their schools.
3. Having students read the book, *Getting into College* (Leana, 1980), which outlines the entire process of the college application, and *The Insider's Guide to Colleges* (Yale Daily News Staff, 1981), which tends to aid students in answering questions about particular schools' programs and campus life.
4. Having students in their third year, interested in gaining first-hand experience in the college search, accompany the teacher-counselor on a six-day tour/visitation to ten Eastern college campuses. This trip affords the prospective college student the opportunity to meet with college admissions officers to discuss curricula related to their special interests, to better understand competition for acceptance to highly selective schools, to ask questions which relate to their individual needs, and to stay with college students in dormitory situations for several nights in order to get a "flavor" of college life and a sense of the school.
5. Having students submit a profile sheet during the senior year with pertinent information on test scores, colleges examined, and those to which the student expects to apply.
6. Reviewing the application procedure for seniors. Considerable time is spent in outlining the process of the interview which is conducted by selective schools. A video tape of Dartmouth College's committee process in screening applicants is shown to demonstrate the need for students to put forth their best effort in the entire application process.
7. Finally, meeting with students, parents, and admissions officers of colleges at mutually acceptable times to review the application process and determine the reasonableness of the students' (and parents') desires related to choice of colleges. These meetings provide the students with the privacy to ask questions which would not be brought up at group meetings, and help parents realize their children's goals.

A graphic model of the components of the counseling program in gifted education at Homewood-Flossmoor High School can be seen in Figure 7.

CONCLUSION

The best evaluation of a program's success is probably made in an examination of the successes of students who leave the program to continue their studies at schools of higher education. In the past

Figure 7. A model high school counseling program for gifted students.

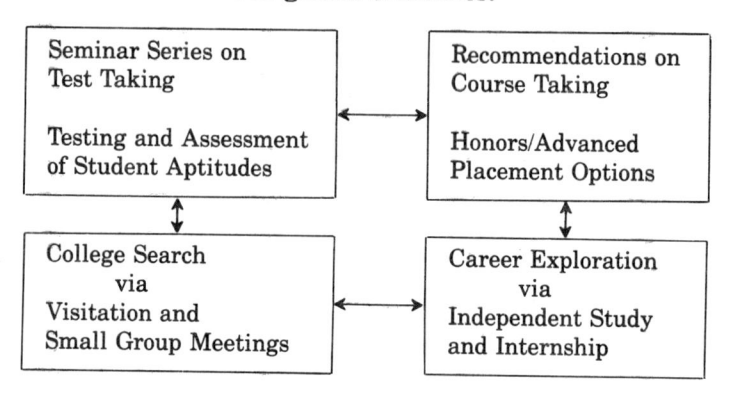

```
┌─────────────────────────┐      ┌─────────────────────────┐
│ Seminar Series on       │      │ Recommendations on      │
│ Test Taking             │      │ Course Taking           │
│                         │◄────►│                         │
│ Testing and Assessment  │      │ Honors/Advanced         │
│ of Student Aptitudes    │      │ Placement Options       │
└───────────▲─────────────┘      └───────────▲─────────────┘
            │                                │
            ▼                                ▼
┌─────────────────────────┐      ┌─────────────────────────┐
│ College Search          │      │ Career Exploration      │
│ via                     │◄────►│ via                     │
│ Visitation and          │      │ Independent Study       │
│ Small Group Meetings    │      │ and Internship          │
└─────────────────────────┘      └─────────────────────────┘
```

twelve years, the number of applications sent by students at Homewood-Flossmoor High School to highly selective schools has quadrupled. In light of the fact that enrollments have decreased by 25% in the same time period, the significance of that trend is even more impressive. More importantly, a greater number of those students are gaining acceptance to these selective schools. For example, only four students were accepted at prestigious institutions in 1980, but in 1981 and 1982, the number increased dramatically—to 50 and 47 respectively.

If the purpose of a gifted program is to prepare students to be successful in academic pursuits and to develop the use of their abilities, then this program has met its goal. The true indication will come when the students served by the program enter their intended professions and become influential in the society they serve.

REFERENCES

Keating, D. P. (Ed.). *Intellectual talent; Research and development.* Baltimore: The Johns Hopkins University Press, 1976.

Leana, F. C. *Getting into college.* New York: Hill and Wang, 1980.

Martinson, R. A. *The identification of the gifted and talented.* Reston VA: The Council for Exceptional Children, 1978.

Passow, A. H. *The gifted and the talented; Their education and development.* Chicago: University of Chicago Press, 1979.

Yale Daily News Staff (Eds.), *The insider's guide to the colleges.* New York: G. P. Putnam's Sons, 1981.